1|24|11
$14.00
I
AS
1 day
2/11

Withdrawn

I1047039

ALSO BY JANCEE DUNN

Don't You Forget About Me: A Novel

*But Enough About Me: A Jersey Girl's
Unlikely Adventures Among the Absurdly Famous*

WHY IS MY MOTHER
GETTING A TATTOO?

WHY IS MY MOTHER GETTING A TATTOO?

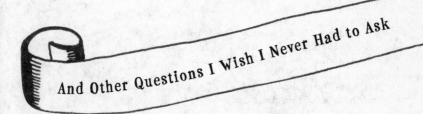

And Other Questions I Wish I Never Had to Ask

Jancee Dunn

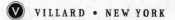

VILLARD · NEW YORK

A Villard Books Trade Paperback Original

Copyright © 2009 by Jancee Dunn

Published in the United States by Villard Books,
an imprint of The Random House Publishing Group,
a division of Random House, Inc., New York.

VILLARD BOOKS and VILLARD & "V" CIRCLED Design are registered
trademarks of Random House, Inc.

Portions of chapter 1, "Triple-Sausage Stuffing with
Sausage Sauce," were originally published in different
form in the August/September 2008 edition of *Modern Bride*.

ISBN 978-0-345-50192-9

Printed in the United States of America

www.villard.com

9 8 7 6 5 4 3 2 1

Book design by Dana Leigh Blanchette

Title page illustrations by Catherine Casalino

CONTENTS

WHY IS MY MOTHER
GETTING A TATTOO?

Triple-Sausage Stuffing
with Sausage Sauce

Recently my younger sister Heather decided to paint her fireplace white. This would be minor news in most families, but not in ours. All day the phone calls flew back and forth. My mother suggested cream instead, which she said was softer. My retiree father phoned from the golf course to warn that painting the fireplace would decrease the property value. I debated the pitfalls of the "wrong" shade of white. My other sister, Dinah, requested a photo of the fireplace before weighing in.

My family does everything by committee, so that the most trivial dilemma is debated with the zeal of Talmudic scholars. (As Dinah puts it, "No one in our family ever says, 'I don't know,' even when they know absolutely nothing about the subject.") We all live within an hour's drive of one another—I'm in Brooklyn, Dinah and my folks live in our home state of New Jersey, and Heather is in a small town in upstate New York—but we can never seem to save these conversations for get-togethers. They require an immediate blizzard of phone calls, so we all signed up for a "friends and family" plan to do it on the cheap.

Dinah, a mild-mannered editor and mother of two, is the most agreeable of our group, and thus most apt to get flattened by the familial steamroller. When she wanted to redecorate her TV room last year, she made the tactical blunder of enthusiastically sharing the plan with Heather and my mother. After weeks of research, she told them, she had picked out two brown couches, a dark brown rug, and, instead of a coffee table, two large tan ottomans.

A short, deadly silence ensued. "Huh," said my mother, a former Southern beauty queen not known for holding back. This is code for *I hate that idea.*

"It'll look like a padded cell," said Heather, the youngest sibling and an elementary school teacher. When I got my first job in New York City, at *Rolling Stone* magazine, a teenage Heather used to covertly run my life, advising me on my career and dating travails, despite having scant experience in either realm.

Dinah, in mid-shrivel, valiantly moved on to plan B. "Okay, instead of the ottomans, how about two little coffee tables that I can move around? That would look kind of cool. Right?" For Dinah, this was a radical proposal.

"When are you going to move them around?" wondered my mother.

"The only time they're going to move," Heather said, "is when your kids run into them and knock them over."

By the end of their little chat, Dinah had been persuaded to get two cream-colored couches, a cream rug with red accents, and a conventional coffee table with clean, modern lines. I saw the results a few weeks later, and while the room looked great, it was leagues away from her original idea.

"Why did you feel compelled to tell them you were redecorating?" I asked.

She shrugged. "Because I really wanted to know what they thought. Sometimes it's nice to be told what's best for you by people who are absolutely sure of their opinions."

"But some of those opinions are half-baked! They just use an emphatic tone of voice so you think they possess some secret knowledge. Hell, I use the same trick. Sometimes as I'm holding forth, I'm thinking, *What the hell am I even* saying?"

Unfortunately, Dinah does not have the lawyerly power of persuasion that the other females of the family specialize in. The longest I've ever witnessed her hold out was twenty minutes. "I never win in family committee meetings," she told me glumly. "Remember my wedding? I kind of remember thinking *I don't know if I want this* a lot. How about the bridesmaids' dresses? You guys wanted red velvet with black trim. I thought you looked like waitresses at Steak and Ale. And Dad insisted I get my hair done at the Penney's beauty salon, and I hated it." My father used to manage the JC Penney in Wayne, New Jersey. "It was poofy and I had ringlets alongside each ear." She sighed. "Ringlets! But I end up conceding. I don't know why. I get on the phone with everyone, and when I hang up, I think, *Whatever.* There are a lot of *whatever*s."

I had to halt the gloomfest. "It's only my wedding," I imitated in a morose voice, ever the domineering eldest sister. "It's only a once-in-a-lifetime event." Why couldn't I resist needling her? Did I always have to revert to being a teen?

"I know what you're trying to do," she broke in. "You're using an Eeyore voice! I am not Eeyore!"

I informed her that she was indeed Eeyore, and she didn't argue with me. Proving my point nicely.

I told her the trick to averting the typhoon of family opinion was to hold off making an announcement until a deed was already done. When Heather found out she was pregnant with her second son, she sent us all an email saying, *We will tell you the baby's name after he is born. In the meantime, we are not accepting any suggestions.* She was still exhausted from the debate around her first child, when names would be glibly rejected for the barest of reasons. We all felt free to condemn any name that reminded us of a classmate from the fourth grade who smelled like fried eggs, or a co-worker who always had crumbs lodged in his goatee and wore stretched-out Shaker-knit sweaters, or someone's cousin who was in the East Jersey State Prison for aggravated assault.

Every name suggestion Heather made was answered with my mother's *Huh,* a sound Heather grew to dread. After a dozen group disputes, Heather and her husband, Rob, warily settled on Travis, which they secretly suspected no one liked. ("Not true," said my mother, reached at home in New Jersey.)

Why do we all allow this boundary-free judgment? It's become a compulsion, one that has grown worse with time so that we now offer our views without any solicitation whatsoever. Who needs an invitation? When my father paid a visit to Dinah's house not long ago, he silently assessed the surroundings, his arms folded across his chest. Having recently ended his thirty-five years of devoted service to Penney's, he had turned his attentions toward preparing his loved ones for anything that could possibly go awry, from financial disaster to termite infestation to scams ("Girls, listen carefully: If someone squirts ketchup or mustard on you, you're being taken for a ride. I saw it on *20/20*").

Dinah braced herself as my father finally cleared his throat. "You know," he began, sounding regretful but firm, "you really need to get these floors redone." Dinah followed him as he walked outside and grimly inspected the grounds. He pointed to the side of the house. "Why haven't you power-washed this area here?"

"Because nobody looks at the side of the house. Including me. I've told you ten times that I don't care."

My father wasn't listening, because he had moved on to the deck's support system, which he deemed "insubstantial," and then to a concrete patch near the garage, which was "crumbling." Before long he had given the place a thorough evaluation and made it clear that it wasn't up to code. His code. He did everything but write up a citation.

"I just invited him over to have lunch," Dinah lamented on the phone to me that night.

Our family opinionfests are the most heated right before Thanksgiving and Christmas, when the holiday menus are negotiated. The calls begin in late October and build to a crescendo by mid-November. Our menu follows the same template every year, but there is just enough variation—a new recipe proposal here, a side-order addition there—that we all feel we must frantically get our bids in, hollering as if we're on the stock market floor. As Heather put it with her usual calm, "If somebody made menu choices without a group consultation, it would be *devastating*." Three years ago, when it became clear that the Magna Carta was drafted with less effort, I announced a streamlined new system: We three siblings would hash out the details in a conference call and report them to the folks. All cautiously agreed.

This year's call clocked in at two hours and twenty minutes. It would have gone longer but Heather's portable phone began to die.

"Why are we doing this?" Dinah complained. "Thanksgiving is always the same damn thing."

"Do you want Heather and me to do this then?" I asked crisply. Order had to be maintained.

Then Dinah threw a bomb. "I made an executive decision without telling anybody," she began. "I bought the gravy."

Silence from Heather and me. "Why did you not clear it?" Heather said finally.

"Because the gravy is fancier than what we normally buy. It was from Whole Foods rather than the crap that Dad buys from ShopRite."

Tempted by the word *fancier,* we assented and moved on to stuffing. There were eight adults at our Thanksgiving table, but no one could agree on flavors, so we had three varieties: traditional bread, corn-bread, and a wild card.

"Patrick wants to make wild-mushroom and chestnut," Dinah ventured.

I snorted. Dinah's meat-loving husband would never make anything vegetarian.

"Please," I said. "Last year he made triple-sausage stuffing with sausage sauce, made from a whole barnyard of different animals. There were maybe two shreds of bread in the whole thing."

"It was not an entire meat stuffing," said Dinah indignantly. "It wasn't a turducken."

After ten minutes we were still deadlocked. "Maybe we should bring a custom stuffing blend for each person," said Heather in exasperation. Finally we agreed on mushroom with a light dose of spicy turkey sausage.

Next we tackled the one lonely green vegetable we would feature. I proposed a new recipe of raw shaved Brussels sprouts with a vinaigrette and Manchego cheese I had seen in a magazine. The girls enthusiastically agreed, murmuring that something fresh and healthy would offset the heaviness of everything else. Then doubt set in.

"It doesn't seem like there's much cheese," Heather pointed out. "No buttered-crumb topping? Maybe we should have creamed spinach instead."

"With lots of cream and cheese," added Dinah. "I want that spinach to barely be green. More like a spinach smoothie."

I sighed. Done. Twenty more minutes were devoted to potatoes (mashed and sweet), rolls (fresh-made and canned crescent rolls, which my father always bought as a backup and then somehow they, too, would make it to the table, so that each person ended up with a pile of a half-dozen rolls). We voted on our usual three pies—chocolate, pecan, and pumpkin. Then Dinah pointed out that my normally recalcitrant husband once agitated for apple pie. "How come he never gets what he wants?" she said. "We have three. Who cares if there's another?"

"It's a little obscene," said Heather. "Four desserts for eight people? That's half a pie for each of us."

"I don't get it," Dinah countered. "If you wanted to make an apple pie for Tom, I wouldn't care. Who cares?"

"Because it's not the way we do it," Heather returned calmly. "Our Thanksgiving would be ruined if there were fruit pies. It's not appropriate. It's not . . ." She searched for the right word. ". . . autumnal."

"Apples aren't autumnal?"

"Why don't we just hold Thanksgiving dinner inside a supermarket?" I broke in. "Then we'll have endless variety."

Wearily we moved on to Christmas dinner, which was at least more streamlined: roast beef and gravy, mashed potatoes with caramelized onions, popovers, and Brussels sprouts, which were somehow appropriate for Christmas and not Thanksgiving. Then Heather and I pushed through the idea of English trifle for dessert, despite Dinah's protestations that it was "like wet, damp cake." To placate her, we added a chocolate cake.

On to lunch. "How about something new?" Dinah said brightly.

A long, skeptical pause followed. "Like what?" Heather said.

"What about something light, like an antipasto spread of

breads and meat and cheeses?" That was our family's idea of "light." Panini were also proposed, and Swedish meatballs, and finally we arrived on sloppy joes. In New Jersey, this isn't the typical ground-beef concoction but a cold sandwich of meat—usually turkey, roast beef, or ham—Russian dressing, Swiss cheese, and coleslaw.

Dinah volunteered to pick them up at the deli near her house. "Hey! What about smoked-turkey joes?" she added.

"I don't get it," I said. "No one makes smoked-turkey joes. You'd order them off the menu? What's wrong with the usual?"

"Why not get gravlax joes?" Heather said with a snicker.

"What's with the cornucopia?" I said. "Enough already."

Dinah was adamant. "It's the holidays, for Christ's sake."

"Take liquid smoke and pour it on your turkey joe then," said Heather. "Dinah. No funny stuff. Don't be buying smoked-turkey joes. Because we'll know. We will know."

"Now I'm worried that you're going to be getting weird-flavored joes," I said. "You remember last year, when we said no to you bringing a pumpkin cake for 'lunch dessert' and you did it anyway? Dinah, do you swear to God you're bringing normal joes?" We made her swear.

As we finally wound down, Dinah mentioned that she had a prolonged sore throat. We asked her a series of questions before briskly diagnosing strep throat, despite neither of us being in possession of a medical degree and my not having even completed my B.A. in English. Then we signed off.

The next morning I wondered if we had been too hard on Dinah, and I called her just to check. "No," she said sunnily. "I think it's sort of funny. Although I do think you and Heather have very similar tastes."

That was true. Because five years separated Heather and me, we never experienced much sibling rivalry, whereas Dinah and I were two years apart. When siblings are significantly younger, they're easier, as children, to bend to your own wishes.

"You two are Frick and Frack," she continued, "and in family meetings, between that and Mom's insane force of will, forget it. When you two obsessively get going about something, I know I've lost."

"But you both turned on me with the Brussels sprouts, and the fondue idea." Heather and I loved to make Dinah sputter, and to make her laugh in spite of herself as she did, but maybe I could relax and allow a fourth stuffing.

And I should have known from grim experience that it's no fun to be at the bottom of a family tackle. When my folks got wind of the fact that Tom and I have separate checking accounts, they brought it up with me the moment I took off my coat during a visit to their house.

"How did you know this?" I asked. I wondered which sibling had ratted me out as my folks soberly delivered a lecture on the symbolism of a joint account, and how it was an investment in our future as a couple.

"Suze Orman says that couples should keep separate checking accounts," I countered. "Do you doubt Suze Orman?"

They traded a dark look that said, *Oh my! Clearly, somebody thinks her marriage won't last!*

"I think the only way to thoroughly learn financial responsibility is to be in charge of your own money," I said. "And we have joint accounts, too. We're bipartisan."

They were unmoved, and I knew full well that after I left, there would be a number of family phone calls behind my back to dissect our loveless, deviant financial arrangement.

But I don't get quite as defensive as I used to when the family spotlight is trained on me. I can pinpoint exactly when it was that I softened: during my wedding a few years ago. Tom and I had announced our engagement at a family dinner. Of course, everyone began chattering at once to tell us exactly what we should do for the ceremony.

The proceedings started out deceptively easy when we reached a speedy consensus on the wedding's location: Sanibel Island, Florida, a sentimental vacation spot for both of our families and the site of Tom's recent proposal. I had been going there for twenty-five years, and it remained the most delightfully corny, wholesome place, with restaurant names like the Hungry Heron and the Lazy Flamingo and retro stores with titles such as She Sells Sea Shells and Three Crafty Ladies.

Then it all slid downhill when we moved on to the menu, and I got a taste of what Dinah went through planning her own wedding. When I proposed the idea of coconut shrimp for appetizers, my hair blew back from the force of the commentary.

Your father doesn't like seafood.

It's Florida so we're having coconut shrimp, end of story!

Forget the shrimp, fried food will kill your appetite.

No, it absorbs alcohol.

Fried shrimp gives me the toots!

Really? Fried shrimp? What about an oyster plate?

Absolutely not. One bad oyster and you'll remember the day for another reason.

Exactly! You'll pray you only get the toots.

Jay, don't be vulgar.

Don't oysters have mercury?

Three hours later, they had endorsed exactly one menu item—steak—and an impassioned debate had broken out around the choice of wedding cake. Fondant icing was vetoed as too brittle, carrot cake as too healthy, spice cake as too risqué. Fresh flower decorations for the cake were nixed because they might contain tiny bugs. To keep everyone happy, Tom and I eventually agreed that each tier would be a different flavor: chocolate, vanilla and raspberry, and lemon coconut. "And don't cut the cake and smash it into each other's faces," said my mother. "It's disgusting, it's not a loving thing to do. Feed each other gently."

"And don't wait too long to serve the cake," said my father. "That always makes people impatient."

"When you say 'people,' do you mean yourself?" I said irritably. "It's going to be just our immediate families, remember?"

"It's only a cake," Tom said later as we drove home. "Why does everything have to be a landmark Supreme Court decision? I don't know how you people get anything done. If this was a corporation, it would be run into the ground."

I sighed. "Get used to it," I said.

And so the months before our wedding were marked by reams of emails. Flowers? "Do all white because it's timeless," Heather wrote. "Colors go in and out of style."

Fine. How about lily of the valley? I suggested in a group—always a group—email.

TOO EXPENSIVE, my father typed back in the capital letters favored by retiree dads. Two dozen emails later, the verdict came in: white roses.

The "long dress or short" discussion grew particularly animated. At first they ruled that I should wear a cocktail dress, because at thirty-five, I was "no spring chicken." Then, in a last-minute nod to tradition, it was voted that I should wear my mother's dress, an unconventional but lovely vintage column of lace.

Should I wear my hair up? Elegant! said my mother. Aging, asserted my sisters. Down is more modern. Exhausted, I compromised with a style of half up, half down by pinning a few front strands back. Take back your wedding, urged my friends. It's about the two of you, not the fourteen of you.

It was too late. As the wedding day approached, Tom and I were down to one decision: the intimate messages we would inscribe to each other on the inside of our wedding rings. When we couldn't agree, Tom teasingly suggested I call my family for advice.

"I already did," I admitted. "They think we should keep it simple and just do dates and initials." He shook his head in resignation.

And so a few weeks later I found myself walking down a sand "aisle" on the beach at Sanibel. When I saw my family's beaming faces, tears blurred my eyes, because I realized that they were having just as much fun as I was. They weighed in on my wedding not to aggravate me but because they shared completely in my happiness. Yes, the ceremony was technically about the joining of two souls, not fourteen, but Tom and I had a lifetime to be a duo. I didn't want to take back my wedding. My family's meddling drove me nuts, but in an increasingly disconnected world, I was actually glad that I had a group of people who cared enough to make twenty phone calls about veil placement.

Of course, everyone has limits. When the wedding was finally over, Tom and I headed back to Brooklyn for a recuperative weekend. Then we began packing for our honeymoon, a long road trip down South.

I held up my cell phone. "Maybe I'll take this, just in case of an emergency," I said casually.

Tom took it gently out of my hands. "No," he said.

2

The Hidden Dangers Lurking
in Your Bathroom Sink

When I picked up my mail this afternoon, I noticed my mother's familiar handwriting on one of the envelopes and knew, without opening it, what it would contain: a newspaper clipping.

"What now," I muttered to my two cats. I work at home alone, so I talk to them a little too often. My cats are my version of office workers—or, if you take a less charitable view, a nutball posse for a semi-deranged person who spends way too much time by herself.

I extracted a clipping titled "Beating Back Nature's Furry Intruders." It was a story about enormous rodents called nutrias, described as "giant rat-like swamp creatures" with "voracious appetites and explosive reproductive capabilities." Originally natives of South America, the article went on, they were imported to the United States in the 1930s for their fur. When they were eventually released into the wild, they started chomping through the wetlands of Louisiana, breeding furiously and invading the entire

Gulf of Mexico. Now they've even been named as a culprit in global warming.

"Who knew?" my mother had scrawled on the top of the paper. I wanted to write my own question, which was "Why are you sending me this?" I don't live near the Gulf of Mexico. I live in New York City, where, as far as I know, there are no wetlands, beyond the streets flooding, and there are already giant rats. What machinations in my mother's brain caused her to read an article on giant rodents and send it to me was a mystery.

But this has been a regular occurrence in my life ever since my parents retired. Over the years it's grown from the occasional bulletin about disease prevention to a veritable deluge of clips. They seem to be a way to say both *Thinking of you* and *Who else but your caring mother would be interested enough in your digestive workings to take the time to send "Five Steps to a Healthy Colon"?* as well as *I may be retired, but as your parent I still have valuable wisdom to dispense, such as this article on litter-box microbes.*

This compulsion to clip 'n' send is a well-known phenomenon among retirees with adult children. One friend of mine from California receives regular clippings from her father from the *Los Angeles Times,* a publication he knows she *already reads every day.* "I think he believes I just skim it," she says with a sigh. "I guess he doesn't want me to miss anything."

The clippings I receive differ slightly, depending on the parent. My mother's are more wide-ranging; my father's are much more predictable, falling under a few general categories:

• *If you don't heed this article, prepare for a grisly mishap in your own home, where you'll use your last breath to wheeze out your address to 911 before you collapse and die.* This would include any and all inflammatory stories on the perils of walking down uncarpeted stairs in socks ("You don't want a nasty fall!" he had scribbled), as well as the importance of having one's chimney cleaned annually to prevent the house from burning down to a few smoking cinders (I don't have a fireplace) and keeping curtains away from electrical outlets, which can shoot out harmful sparks (I have blinds, not curtains). Over the years, I've received warnings in the mail about "deadly household tragedies" such as unattended candles falling on the rug and setting an entire house ablaze in seconds; carelessly ingesting cough medicine without checking the expiration date; having a faulty seal in your refrigerator door, which can encourage hazardous bacteria growth; and cooking in loose clothing, which can easily burst into flames and turn you into a screaming, capering fireball. Usually these missives are accompanied by a cheery, reassuring note like "Remember that accidents can happen anytime, anywhere! XO, Dad." If the headline contains the word *lurking* ("The Hidden Dangers Lurking in Your Bathroom Sink/Artificial Sweeteners/Dog's Ears/Home's Foundation/Tea Bags"), then he feels he has done his job.

• *If you don't buy this item from my favorite catalog, Improvements, with its not-at-all-hectoring slogan, "There's always something around your house that could use Improvements," well, then, best of luck to you. Best of luck.* Products that are carefully marked with my father's treasured highlighting pen might include fingerprint-activated door locks, mattress protectors that shield you from gangs of marauding dust mites, and something called a Blackout Home Safety Kit. Heather tells me that my father recently paid her a visit and was horrified to discover her bathroom window did not have any sort of curtains or blinds. Arriving promptly in the mail was a clipping from Improvements offering a classy, opaque stick-on film that fitted over the window. ("Will put off those Peeping Toms!" my father had scribbled.)

Finally, if my dad finds out that I am buying any sort of appliance, or thinking about purchasing a new car, or considering any form of home upgrade whatsoever, a sheaf of cuttings from *Consumer Reports* will reliably show up in the mail. My father carefully files his *Consumer Reports* to prepare for the emergency of one of his daughters blithely buying a product that has not been rated number one by *Consumer Reports*' impartial testing lab.

Tom and I recently decided that we were going to get a new refrigerator and, after a little research, had settled on one brand, but of course I couldn't commit until I had vetted our choice with my father. Imagine my alarm when I caught Tom cavalierly dialing up the appliance store one day to check prices. "Whoa, whoa, whoa," I said when he hung up the phone. "Do you want to break my father's heart? Do you?"

He laughed. "But I already went online and *Consumer Reports* approves of this brand."

"Tom. Please."

Mechanically, he dialed my folks' number. "Hi, Jay," he said woodenly. "How are you? Oh, the Giants are on? Who's winning?"

Ask him! I mouthed, making my eyes bulge out in what I hoped was a menacing manner.

"Listen, we're thinking of buying a new fridge, and we wanted to know if you had any thoughts." Oh, yes, my father most definitely had some thoughts. "Mm-hmm," said Tom. "Right. Uh-huh. Mm-hmm. Right. Yes. Right. Hadn't thought of that. Well, I was wondering if you might have any *Consumer Reports* lying around that feature the best refrigerators."

"Why, of course!" I heard my father say happily.

Tom looked at me. "He's going to get his files," he whispered.

"Thank you," I whispered back.

My mother, meanwhile, tends to send ideas that she harvests

for me to write about in magazines, some of which have proven to be useful (a recent clip was about a new kind of recumbent bike, noted with "So interesting!"). Other categories include:

• *Funny!!!:* This is a broad human-interest category, often culled from community newspapers, but the common thread is that my mother will scribble "Funny!!!" on the top. Animals behaving badly are always a hit, because my suburban folks see the natural world as something to subdue and love when a rebellious creature gets its comeuppance. (Recent headlines: "Woman Gets into Tussle with Aggressive Deer" and "Raccoon's Crime Spree Finally Comes to an End.") But it can also include humans behaving badly, especially if an "area nude man" is discovered mowing his lawn, or holding up a convenience store, or cheerfully driving a golf cart. ("Dummy!" my mother will scrawl gleefully.) If something unusual is being deep-fried at a state fair (Twinkies! Pickles! Oreos!), I will read about it. If a report surfaces on a hamster who saves a family trapped in an overturned car, into the envelope it goes.

• *Inspirational:* "Dying breeds" are popular with my mother ("Newark Family Doctor Still Makes House Calls"). So are stories of an entire town rallying around some down-and-out person, or the tale of a wizened ninety-five-year-old woman who still shows up early every day to work as a secretary in an elementary school and enjoys a daily double martini afterward (obligatory quotes about meeting President Calvin Coolidge as a girl a bonus).

• *Completely and utterly irrelevant to my life:* "Celebrity-Inspired Drinks Not Always Toastworthy." I don't go to bars. That's because I don't drink. So I wouldn't order a cocktail, whether it's celebrity-inspired or not. "Raw-Food Diet Has Pros and Cons." I've never been on a raw-food diet. That's because I like my food cooked.

For any parent, clippings can conveniently substitute for discussions they'd rather not have. A recently divorced friend of mine just received a torrent of clips from her mother on the exciting joys and high effectiveness rate of Internet dating. And my folks know they can only push me so far in their relentless quest for a grandchild, so an inflammatory headline that childless women are more likely to get breast cancer furthers their cause nicely without bringing up the issue directly. As medical fearmongering is a consistent theme of these missives, they can innocently claim that they just want me to live for a long time—is that such a crime?

One night Dinah phoned. "You know how Dad keeps trying to convince me to tell Patrick to get a gastric lap band?"

"Yes." Her husband, Patrick, has been fighting his weight forever. Making matters worse, he's a chef. With diabetes.

"Ever since Dad saw a segment on *60 Minutes* about how it can stop diabetes, he's been obsessed. But he never tells Patrick, he tells me. And I keep fending him off by saying that Patrick's trying to lose weight on his own. But Dad couldn't wait, because a clipping just arrived for Patrick about laparoscopic surgery."

"Dad meant well. It's like his phantom form of communication."

She sighed. "I know. But I like the articles about Roth IRAs better, or that one about the pig that likes to go surfing."

I can't bring myself to toss out some of these little pieces of paper, so I often save them until they're yellow. They're stuffed in a drawer in my bedside table, and one of them, a collection of lucky numbers that my mother sent me to play Lotto, falls out of my wallet every time I pull out some cash. I suppose these clips are a way of maintaining a bond with a nonstop flow of the comfortingly mundane. Most are about everyday matters, the sorts of ordinary things that I would discuss a lot more if I lived closer, rather than in the next state, and could just drop by for a visit (whereas when I chat with my folks on the phone, we tend to stick to the big topics). It's a way for us to pretend we live in the same neighborhood—which, by the way, my father would love. Many times when I have visited them, he has taken me for a morning spin around their New Jersey town to point out the houses for sale that I might like. (Then I return home to a torrent of clippings from the real estate section of his paper, with wheedling notes in the margins that say things like "Check out this state-of-the-art kitchen! Open house this Sunday if you want to see it in person. I'll pick you up at the train station!")

After a clip has been mailed by either parent, I often get a phone call to ascertain that the clip was received. The other day, when my father phoned to inquire if I had any thoughts about the article he sent on early retirement planning, I asked him why he felt the need to send so many clippings.

"Generally, I find information in an area you don't read about," he said. "No matter how old or mature my daughters are, I think you might have missed something. And obviously I'm worried about you, about your safety. At your age, you think you're immortal, and thank goodness. At my age you're trying not to slip and break a hip. I guess as you get older, you anticipate things like that more. When you're younger, your tendency is to react to a situation, but when you get older, you're in the preventative stage. So I try, as much as I can, to ward off bad things from happening, both to me and to you girls—try to prevent things two moves out, as chess players say.

"Like the crank radio that I keep telling you girls to buy," he continued. *Oh, no. Here we go. Not the crank-radio speech again.* "I bought one, as you know, and I really think everyone else should have one, too." *Here comes the phrase "substantial power outage." I can feel it. It is coming 'round the corner.* Predicting the next phrases he will use is a helpful mental game for staying awake when he goes on one of his jags. "If there's a substantial power outage or a national emergency, most radio stations will be operated on generators. The only way you'll hear them will be with a crank radio. How are you supposed to get your information otherwise? You're completely cut off."

"You're right, Dad." As I hung up, I felt a little sheepish. As much as my sisters and I made fun of him and Mom for their eye-roll-inducing clippings, it was clear that my father was genuinely plagued by the thought that I might be trapped somewhere, surrounded by rubble, with no way of knowing what's going on. If he couldn't live near me to race to the rescue, then this was the best backup plan he could manage.

And, God help me, I've begun to clip, too. Last year I read an irritating article in the *Wall Street Journal* on home owners who install a second laundry room in their McMansions in order to save themselves the bother of actually walking up or down the stairs to wash their clothes. *Ugh,* I thought, reaching for the scissors.

"Do you believe this?" I wrote on the top, adding a new "What will people do next?" category to our family clipping oeuvre. Then I stuck it in an envelope, which I addressed to my folks.

"Just this once," I said to the cats.

3

They Don't Make Designer Colostomy Bags

My father has spent his entire adult life surrounded by strong women. In family portraits, he always looks happy but a little dazed. Our cats were females. We even had a lady hamster. With little escape for him beyond trips to the hardware store and quality time with his beloved television, no wonder his annual golf trip was so eagerly anticipated.

Every spring for the past twenty years, my father has headed for Myrtle Beach with a genial herd of twenty fellow JC Penney managers. Now retirees, they bunk four per condo, and for a solid week their routine stays comfortingly unvaried. The festivities commence at sunrise with a long stretch of golf, then a brief break for lunch, followed by more golf, capped by a rejuvenating nap. In the late afternoon they gather in their respective condos for men's versions of appetizers: mixed nuts and snack mix. Over the years, each group developed a signature predinner snack, and my father's condo, thanks to his tireless campaigning, wowed the competition with gin and tonics and microwave popcorn. Their appetites whetted, the whole aftershave-scented, Dockers-and-Greg-Norman-shirted gang goes to dinner, where company gossip and shop talk about JC Penney is energetically exchanged. After dessert and decaf, they rise from their chairs, announce to one another that "it doesn't get any better than this," and head off to bed, some of them donning earplugs to block the noisy snoring of their condo mates. Then they get up to do it all again.

This past spring my father arranged a double dose of fun for himself when a smaller group of different JC Penney retirees—coed this time—descended on Charleston the week before his golf jamboree. For him, the only thing more blissful than a week of talking about JC Penney is two weeks of talking about JC Penney. My mother accompanied him to Charleston, less for the Penney's conclave and more for the shrimp and grits. In need of a getaway, I arranged to meet them both in Savannah, at which point my father would journey to Myrtle Beach, while my mother and I would spend our first long weekend together alone.

When my husband, Tom, and I traveled, he adamantly refused to do historic-house tours, which he called deadening experiences (even as he fed his own interest in relics of the Cold War, dragging me through abandoned missile silos and the former headquarters of the East German secret police). During the few times I was able to bring Tom along, his face had the same sour expression that my childhood Siamese cat wore when I dressed it up in doll's clothes. "What am I going to learn about a historical figure by looking at his chamber pot in some dismal roped-off area?" he would grumble. Well, my mother and I loved looking at chamber pots. I remembered with fondness a trip to the Dickens home in London, where I gazed, transfixed, at the great man's commode.

I booked a flight to Savannah and began planning. I was a little nervous, because I wanted my mother to have the time of her life. Until the morning I left, I was still planning furiously.

I knew my parents would be parked at the arrivals area because they had confirmed it with me four times. Parents love to reconfirm a reconfirmation.

"Hey, kid!" said my father from the front seat of their car as I hopped into the back, which was instantly familiar: the pile of books on tape, the matching towels to protect their clothing when they ate in the car, the jumbo pack of bottled water and energy bars, the spare rolls of quarters and breath mints.

"Hah, honey," said my mother. Her Southern accent had returned in full force. It happened every time my Alabama-born mom crossed the Mason-Dixon line: Within minutes she was once again a Daughter of the Southland. Her drawl deepened, her pace slowed, her smile widened as she drank in the humid, magnolia-scented air and transformed from quick-moving Northerner to General P. G. T. Beauregard.

My father turned around, concerned. "Have you got the directions to the hotel?"

"Yes." I produced a printout from a folder marked "Savannah." Truly, I was my father's daughter. We both loved making folders and filing them in neat rows inside pristine file cabinets with color-coordinated labels.

"Well, good!" he said, passing it to my mother. "Hey, kid, did you get that funny email I sent you yesterday? The one from Vern Leister?"

I received many, many, many, many forwarded emails from Vern, one of my father's Penney's cronies, but I knew precisely the one he was talking about, because it was my father's favorite sort of email. Vern's header was *Sure brought back a lot of memories,* followed by forty-two pictures of items from days gone by: S&H

Green Stamps, a series of roadside signs for Burma Shave, Lincoln Logs, a pile of penny candy . . . And no postwar nostalgia collection would be complete without a black-and-white photo of Marlin Perkins, host of *Mutual of Omaha's Wild Kingdom*.

"I thought you'd be interested," he said. "Your generation didn't experience some of this great stuff. Did you see the picture of Old Yeller? It was one of those feel-good movies of the time."

Feel-good? I reminded him that the harrowing scenes of a snarling, rabid Old Yeller being shot dead by his tearful young owner made me feel distinctly bad when I saw it as a kid, but his gauzy memory only retained the earlier scenes of a frisky Old Yeller frolicking through the fields, his eyes clear, his muzzle free of rabies foam.

"Every Saturday afternoon we'd go to the movies," continued my father mistily. "It was something all the kids did in those days. You'd pay ten cents for a movie and five for popcorn. Man, I looked forward to those movies all week. They were gentler times." He shook his head and smiled. The man actually enjoyed all of Vern's missives: *World's Scariest Bridges* ("AND YOU THOUGHT THE GOLDEN GATE BRIDGE WAS FRIGHTENING!!!" Vern had typed); *Something to Make You Smile* (a mother pig nursing five puppies, a giant Saint Bernard and a kitten snoozing peacefully together); or the ever-popular *This will blow your mind* (a card trick that *magically picked the very card you were thinking of*). Inevitably my father asked me about them later, which is why I could never delete his email forwards, dutifully reading each one and writing back a comment like "How about that?"

"Folks, I have to tell you that sometimes I don't know which one of you is sending me an email," I said. "You two are growing together like an old tree."

"Hm," said my mother. "I know: I'll sign each email with an X. No, a double X. That'll be my trademark."

"And I'll sign it with two O's," decided my father.

My mother frowned. "No, Jay. Don't sign it with anything. Just leave it blank. I'll do double X and that's how the girls will know the difference between us."

"But why can't I have a signature too? I want double O's."

"It's too confusing! Why do you need double O's? I don't know why you're so adamant about this, I—"

Their argument could easily have stretched to ten minutes if I didn't do something. Lord have mercy, it was going to be a long weekend. "Excuse me," I broke in, "but is anyone paying attention to where we're going?"

My mother rustled the direction sheet and looked up sharply. "Jay, we're about to miss the turn." Thirty minutes and four squabbles later, my parents had piloted us to the Gastonian hotel, a lavish Regency mansion where I had spent my honeymoon. I had booked one of the only two rooms with twin beds. My mom and I had rarely done anything like this together, so I wanted it to be perfect.

My father lugged my mother's gargantuan suitcase up the stairs and dragged it to the front desk, where a preoccupied young woman sat.

"Well, hello there!" my father cried.

"Hello, sir," she said, putting down some paperwork. "I'm sorry, I was just finishing up some forms for my mother. She is applying for U.S. citizenship."

"Well, isn't that nice?" said my dad. "Where is she from?"

"Haiti."

"Oh." My father's smile vanished. "There's so much turmoil over there, I hope she gets out okay."

I fidgeted as my parents quizzed her about her family. My folks chatted, at length, with everyone: waiters, people in elevators, young mothers with strollers. *Maybe the clerk has stuff to do,* I fretted. *There could be a time limit for those forms to be submitted, and the minutes are ticking away, and then her mother will have to stay in Haiti forever. Stop talking!*

But the clerk seemed perfectly happy to answer my folks' questions and volley back their jokes. I willed myself to relax. Not everyone was in a perpetual hurry.

We checked in, stowed our luggage, and got right back into the car for the first stop on my airtight itinerary, Bonaventure Cemetery. Oh, how we Dunns love graveyards. We started wandering among the moss-covered tombstones and grand old trees draped with soft Spanish moss. Aside from one German couple, we were the only people in the cemetery, which was often the case.

"Ooh, look at this one." My mother stood in front of a moldering tombstone chiseled with the words LOST AT SEA. Nearby was another grave with a disconsolate white-marble angel clinging to the side. That was my kind of tombstone. I wanted a weeping statue, overcome with grief at my passing, for all eternity.

I gradually drifted to a far corner of the cemetery, lost in romantic fantasies as I sat on a carved stone bench while the wind gently stirred the live oaks around me. What if you could pry open some of the coffins? Would you find bits of silk from burial dresses, heavy old rings, strands of hair from all of the Elizas and Josiahs? Would their skeletal hands be clutching a musty keepsake—a small Bible, a daguerreotype of a loved one? What if you opened the lid and the person's face was magically intact, fresh as life, before the air caused it to disintegrate? Within minutes, it would be gone, *except in your dreams.*

My idyll was broken as a car slowly pulled up behind me. It was my father, who tired of all activities after exactly one hour. No matter where we were—a museum, a shopping center—once that hour passed, he would announce that he'd wait for us outside and go park himself on a bench. You could never continue shopping or gazing at art without thinking of him grimly waiting like a tied-up spaniel.

He rolled down the car window. *Zzzt.* "The place closes down in twenty minutes," he said with a concerned frown. "We'd better get ready to go." The exit was six yards away. I could see it from where I stood. And what did he mean, "get ready"? Pack provisions? Saddle up?

"I'm not done yet," I said over my shoulder as I made my way toward a particularly haunting statue of a lamb, or was it a dog? Slowly the car glided behind me. I tried shooing him away like a chicken, but it was no use. He remained nearby with the engine idling until I gave up with a sigh and got into the car.

We drove back to the hotel to freshen up for dinner and then took a walk to Chippewa Square. I asked them on the way if we could make a quick stop at the drugstore. For starters, I'd forgotten my sunblock, which was a disaster, as I have very thin skin, like a newt. "And to be frank, I don't feel myself today," I told them.

My mother stopped on the sidewalk. "What's the problem?" she demanded. She took my chin into her hand and squinted at me, aiming my head at different angles.

"Wrong end," I said.

My father put down the map he was studying. "You mean you're not going to the bathroom?" he announced loudly as a nearby tour group peered at me with concern.

"This is just the second day," I said in a low voice, hoping he'd follow suit.

Obstructed bowels happened to be a subject that worked my father into a frenzy of fearmongering. "You get impacted!" he thundered. "You want fecal impaction? Days go by, you let that fester long enough in your bowels, and it'll turn into a *rock*. You think you can pass a rock? Well, you'd better call the *Guinness Book of World Records,* because you'd be the first person to do it."

"I could be wrong, but I don't think fecal rock passing is an official category for them."

"You think this is funny? Next thing you know, you're off to the hospital to get it surgically removed. Is that what you want? You think giving birth hurts? That's a walk in the park compared to getting your impacted feces taken out."

My mother narrowed her eyes at him. "Jay, how the hell would you know? Men always like to downplay the pain of childbirth. I had three of *your* children, and let me tell you, each time I was paralyzed from the neck down, and still I screamed for more drugs. Hell, if someone had put a knife in my hand, I would have performed my own C-section."

He ignored her. "You better thank your lucky stars you don't get colon cancer!" he boomed at me. "Gotta keep it moving, or all that toxic waste sits around in your intestine, eats away the walls of your colon, and pretty soon you're pooping in a bag! You want that? Because I got a news flash for you, they don't make designer colostomy bags." My father dearly loved to deliver "news flashes."

My mother put a hand on his arm. "Let's find a drugstore. I think there's one on Bull Street. Jay, you wait here." She marched me to the pharmacy, heading straight to the Aisle of Shame, which offered relief for every ailment that itches, burns, or oozes out of the lower half of your body. "Here we go," she said, picking up a plastic container. "Stool softener," she read loudly. "Huh. You might be past that point, if you've got a fecal rock." As embarrassing as it was, I couldn't help but get a little sentimental. Who but your mom cares about your bowels?

"Could you keep it down?" I said. "And just because Dad says I have a fecal rock in my lower intestine doesn't mean I actually have one, or that this condition even exists in the first place. Dad's not a doctor, remember? He's a former JC Penney manager." My father gleaned most of his medical news from reports on the CBS *Sunday Morning* show. Mix in a little thirdhand information from golf buddies and a soupçon of Internet rumor, and suddenly the walls of your colon are being "eaten away."

My mother held up another jar. "Castor oil," she said. "Mama used to give me a spoonful of that stuff every morning. Lord, did that taste awful. It does keep you regular, though."

"Why don't you announce it on the loudspeaker?"

She picked up another box. "Ooh! Enemas! How about one of these? They work right quick."

"Mom? You don't need to read each label aloud."

She was obviously enjoying my squirming. "Look at this! Who knew they still made milk of magnesia?"

I grabbed a box of Ex-Lax. "Let's go. Will you buy it? I'll wait by the door."

"Oh, for Christ's sake. Who are you going to run into in Savannah?" But she did it, as I waited outside with my father on a bench.

After dinner, my dad dropped us at the Gastonian and continued on to a roadside motel so he could leave early for Myrtle Beach. We raced up to our room to inspect it, stopping first in the lobby. "Oooh, free wine!" my mother cried. She poured it so enthusiastically that it slopped over the top of her glass.

In the room she ran over to the bed. "Look, they put a praline on our pillow!" my mother said delightedly. "Maybe they'll give us more stuff tomorrow." She opened a desk drawer. "I'll take this pen and put it in my purse. Then maybe they'll replace it." Inwardly I beamed like a lighthouse that she approved of the place. She has hated an entire guidebook's worth of B and Bs. "Charming and quaint," to her, meant thin walls, saggy beds, and tepid coffee.

She briskly unloaded the contents of three large plastic bags, covering the entire bathroom counter with Soft & Dri antiperspirant in Kissed Peach, makeup-remover towelettes, and three generous containers of prescription pills.

I picked up one bottle. "Why so many pills?"

"There are only three."

"No, there are four."

She looked at the fourth bottle. "Sleepin' pills don't count." *Au contraire, lady,* I thought. *Sleepin' pills most definitely count, especially when you wash them down with a few glasses of Pinot Noir and start speaking in tongues and tearing strips of wallpaper off the walls, as you are wont to do.*

Before bed, she set up her travel-sized white-noise machine. Every member of our family, including my two-year-old nephew, possesses a noise machine of his very own. I was the last holdout. White noise always makes me jumpy. I can never fall asleep on an airplane because of the ambient noise and am always the lone passenger on an overnight flight who remains awake, glumly reading *Us* magazine under a tiny pool of light while everyone else snoozes around me, heads thrown back obliviously, mouths gaping. But my husband was determined to get one, insisting that the drunken revelers in our Brooklyn neighborhood made too many whooping noises on the weekends as they spilled out of bars.

"If there's silence, I'll just sit and imagine that I'm going to hear a noise, and it will bother me," he said, using some sort of vague Klingon logic. "The silence calls more attention to the fact that there will be a noise that will inevitably come."

Eventually he wore me down. "The nicest models have actual nature sounds," he said. "We can use the rainstorm noise. Who doesn't like to sleep during a nice rainstorm?" And so one morning a pricey contraption called Tranquil Moments arrived in the mail. It offered a jarring array of sounds that were the opposite of tranquil: frogs croaking, a lashing thunderstorm, the lonely cry of disoriented gulls.

Tom eagerly opened the box and started fiddling with the machine. We explored the panel of soundscapes before settling on Harbor, with a foghorn that seemed fairly soothing until we realized that unlike the real thing, it blatted every three seconds.

"Look, you can mix two noises, like you're a deejay," he said. "See? You can make a mash-up. Let's try Frogs, and . . . hm . . . how about Crackling Fire?" The combination sounded like the poor creatures were croaking helplessly while being roasted alive.

He hastily changed the dial. "What about Ocean Surf and Thunderstorm?" I pictured a sailor lost at sea, struggling to gain control of his craft before plunging over the side into the icy water, spinning down, down, down, his mouth open in a silent scream.

Tom sighed and gave the dial another twiddle. "How about Generator?" He turned up a muted humming noise. "We can mix it with Rainforest," he added, blending in the sound of water gently pattering on leaves. I pictured oil machinery and pipelines chugging ominously away in the formerly pristine Guatemalan rainforest. The only sound missing was that of squawking animals fleeing in terror.

We finally settled on the stream noise, which was not a cheerful trickle but a mighty flow suitable for class-five kayakers. It compelled me to visit the bathroom four times a night, but at least I was used to it, so I had my mother switch her noise machine to

Stream rather than her customary Waterfall. Then I went into the bathroom to put on my pajamas while she donned hers in the bedroom.

When I came out, I stared at her in disbelief. We were wearing the same flannel numbers from LL Bean that are sold every Valentine's Day. Covered with candy hearts that say things like TRUE LOVE and (my favorite) FAX ME, they are the perfect combination of comfortable and cheerfully deranged, to the head-shaking resignation of my husband. They would only be alluring to a man who had a thing for his Aunt Mabel. No wonder I hadn't given my parents any grandchildren.

Granted, mine were white and hers were pink, but I had noticed that lately our tastes were fusing into one pink-and-white, candy-heart-studded ball. When we had taken the jaunt through the cemetery, we both inspected the tombs with our hands on our hips angled in just the same way before I saw what was happening and quickly folded my arms. And when did I start to get as excited as she did about new cleaning products? *It's happening,* I thought. *Oh, Lord, it is happening.* Adulthood comes not with the realization that you're turning into your mother but with the acceptance of it. At this stage in our lives, I was forced to admit that we were much more alike than we were different.

"What's different?" asked my mother. I realized I had spoken aloud—another thing that my mother does all the time.

"What? Oh, nothing."

She shrugged and took out her contacts, downed a sleepin' pill, put in industrial-strength earplugs, and pulled the covers completely over her head, as is her habit. With her burrowed in like a badger under the blankets, all I could see of her was a tuft of Medium Ash Blonde hair poking out at the top. I read my book with all the lights in the room blazing. She didn't even turn over, which was a relief. She had always been a light sleeper and woke with a volley of obscenities to any noise. When we were younger, I learned to navigate the squeaky floorboards of our hallway by creeping along the edge of the walls to the bathroom. I had no desire to revisit that time.

Type A even on vacation, we bounded out of bed early the next morning so that we could cram in three house tours. "That tile floor is slippery, just so you know," my mother said as she emerged from the bathroom clad in a towel. "I stepped out of the shower and nearly fell on my *kazatz*." Sometimes she made up her own form of Methodist Yiddish.

Off we went to the Andrew Low House near Lafayette Square. On the way my mother, crisp and polished in slim black pants and a white top, noted with approval the ladylike dresses she saw on the locals. She had a cringe-inducing habit of commenting on passersby as if she were safely behind a two-way mirror. "Look at all the pretty colors!" she said. "Southern women just look a little more polished." Conversely, she was aghast at some of the sloppy outfits on the tourists. "Gracious, look at the ankles on that woman," she said, pop-eyed with horror at a blonde who stood two feet away from us. "And she's wearing capri pants, of all things!"

My mother, while naturally pretty, puts a lot of zeal into looking good. Her hair is always perfectly styled and highlighted. The only time I ever see her without lipstick is well before breakfast. Every January, she methodically diets to lose any trace of holiday weight. Thus, for this jaunt I left my casual getups at home and packed more carefully to escape her laser up-and-down gaze.

To my silent horror, I soon learned that house tours with my mother were more of a call-and-response situation. The last thing I wanted was a group of strangers gawping at me, but my mother couldn't care less, having often told me that one of the joys of getting older was not giving a "hoot" what people thought. "Andrew

Low's most famous guest was Robert E. Lee, who stayed in this bedroom," said the guide mechanically, standing in front of a canopied bed.

"Well, isn't that interestin'," murmured my mother, who had dropped her *g*'s and left them somewhere up north. My palms started to sweat.

"He was a houseguest here for a week," the guide continued.

"Huh," said my mother loudly, causing a few people to turn around. She looked at a picture of Robert E. Lee that was proudly displayed on the bedroom wall. "He really was a handsome man," she announced, and others around us nodded.

"Meanwhile, General William Tecumseh Sherman, who of course burned Atlanta, spared our fair city of Savannah, giving it to President Abraham Lincoln as a Christmas present." The guide went on to explain that instead, Sherman seized the cotton that was languishing in cargo ships to use up north.

My mother put up her hand. "Well, did he pay for it?"

The guide snorted. "What do you think?"

My mother put her hands on her hips. "Those Yankees," she said disgustedly, and the group chortled. Everyone else seemed to be entertained by her, while a part of me always remained a pained, self-conscious teen in her presence. I refrained from mentioning that she currently lived in New Jersey. Northern New Jersey.

After another house tour, we broke for lunch. Her accent guaranteed that we were never consigned to the tourist ghetto in restaurants. "Hah theyah!" she would chirp brightly. "D'y'all have a nice table fuh two? You do? Why, thenk yew!"

We spent the day indulging in every feminine activity that we could possibly do short of tampon shopping. We hit an antique garden furniture store, made a stop for cupcakes and lemonade, breezed into a stationery and note card emporium, and walked through a garden before racing back to the hotel in time for the free late-afternoon wine. Then it was off to a soothing 6 P.M. dinner of shrimp and grits. As we strolled home, she stopped in the middle of the sidewalk.

"Dawg gone it!" she cried. She really does say "dawg gone it." "I haven't called your father yet." She rummaged through her purse and produced her cell phone. "Dammit," she said, peering at the screen. "He's called me four times already." This was typical. As usual when he was away from her, my father had logged many mournful calls while she had been busy laughing and clinking lemonade glasses with me.

My mother had instilled in all of us girls the ability to enjoy our own company, and the men in our lives were often baffled by how little they were missed when we were elsewhere.

"Hi, Jay," she said dutifully. "Uh-huh. Mm-hm. Well, your golf game is never good the first day. You always get better. You know that." Then she perked up. "You watched Oprah? With all of the guys around? Well, how did you manage that?"

My father had always rolled his eyes at my mother's daily Oprah fix, but in the preceding year, after they'd received TiVo as a Christmas present, she'd started recording the show and watching it during dinner. Gradually my father, usually a fan of gory crime shows and New York Giants games, became a convert, going from grumbling about that "touchy-feely crap" to holding forth at the dinner table about the wonder and magic of *The Oprah Winfrey Show.* "I'm not into the ones about the giveaways and stuff, some of your more lightweight ones like kitchen remodeling and makeovers and what have you, but I tell you, that Oprah has a number of programs that are fascinating. Real human-interest stuff, like *CBS News Sunday Morning* does."

And so after a round of golf, my father had tiptoed off to his bedroom to watch Oprah's interview with Barbara Walters. Initially his condo mates had a good chuckle, but soon enough, two of them had pulled up a chair. My mother shook her head as she hung up the phone. "I'm not surprised that all of his cronies joined in. Park a man on a couch, turn on a television, and he'll watch anything. Hell, that's how I got your father to watch Oprah in the first place. It was easier for him to sit there than to get up and move to another room."

The next day sped by as we quickly made our way through my roster of activities. She seemed as determined as I was to make this a capital-*M* memory. As soon as we finished one thing she would ask me what was next as I shuffled worriedly through my folder. My father traditionally assumed the navigational duties when they were together. Now it was up to me.

Before we knew it, we found ourselves back at the hotel for the appetizers and the "free" libations—wine for her, sweet tea for me, which we carried to a shaded arbor at the back of the hotel.

"Good, there's nobody here," said my mother, inspecting the area. "Let's sit on this porch swing."

We took a seat and listened to the birds chirping. "Did you call Tom today?" she asked.

"I did, while you were in the shower."

She took a sip of wine. "Aren't you glad you married him? Your father and I always say, 'Thank God for Tom.'"

"I'm glad every day," I said.

"If something happened to Tom, do you think you'd remarry?"

I shook my head. "I don't know, Ma. I doubt it. It took me long enough to find *him*. We're talking decades."

"I feel the same way. I think I'm more of a picky person than your father is. I always think about what my sister Juanita said after her husband Joe died. She said she'd never get married again, because all old geezers were looking for was a nursemaid. But listen, if I croak before your father does—"

"Please," I interrupted her. "You're one of those people who will hang on with both fingernails until you're in the triple digits."

She ignored me and tipped back some more wine. "If I croak before he does, it's up to you girls to get him a new wife."

I sat up. "Really?" We had never had this discussion before, but I found, to my surprise, that it wasn't upsetting. I was comforted, like her, by the idea of having a plan. Not that she was ever going to die, of course.

"Yes, and sooner rather than later. You don't even have to wait a year. Six months, that's fine. He says he could never remarry, but I don't want him to be unhappy. And Lord knows there are a lot of predatory gals out there. He would have no problem whatso-ever. Let's face it, the numbers favor the men. And he's the type of person that needs somebody else around."

I nodded. "True."

"Grandchildren and kids, it's not the same. You don't tell your children the same things you would talk about with your spouse. You don't sleep with your grandchildren and kids, either."

I didn't know precisely what to say to that, just as I didn't know how to respond earlier, at lunch, when she remarked that every generation thinks that they invented oral sex. So I quickly changed the subject and asked her what she wanted to do on our last night in town.

"Ooh! I know," she said, brightening. "I want to go on a 'Haunted Savannah' ghost tour! There was a brochure in the lobby. Why don't I call and see if I can get us in?"

I told her I was not a tour aficionado, but she gradually per-suaded me. ("Oh, come on, aren't you the least bit curious? What if it's *really spooky*?") And so as night fell, we walked over to the parking lot of a nearby café and waited for the guide.

A minivan soon pulled up and a middle-aged man climbed out. I saw my mother's face fall when she spotted his rainbow suspenders. When it comes right down to it, there are not many positive situations that involve rainbow suspenders. The first date or new boss that bounces in wearing rainbow suspenders evokes a major "uh-oh" moment. Think about it: Mork from Ork. Steve Urkel. Mimes. One exception might be the hired entertainment at a children's party, but even then, those suspenders let you know exactly what you're in for.

The man explained that he was an actor who had once appeared as a ghoul in *Dawn of the Dead*. Then two other people ran up, breathless, and we were ready to go. He retrieved his walking stick from the minivan, and we proceeded to the first haunted house.

He stood in front, leaning on his stick in what he thought was a picturesque way, and told us about a nineteenth-century girl who had been punished by her father for naughtiness by being tied to a chair in front of the parlor window for three days before she expired. His timing was off, and his tale did not contain the barest trace of spookiness. When he started re-creating scenes using different dialects—another worrisome flag—my mother officially turned on him and lagged grumpily behind the group as we made our way to the next house.

He pointed to the soaring Cathedral of Saint John the Baptist, to the glittering gold cross atop the spire, and mentioned that someone had climbed it in the nineties to steal the cross, before firemen were summoned to lead the hapless criminal down.

My mother craned her neck to see the top of the spire. "It seems pretty high for a person to climb," she said doubtfully. The guide ignored her. She turned to me. *I don't like him*, she mouthed. *I want my money back.* I silently thanked the Lord that this wasn't my idea and my record remained unblemished.

As he continued with his tour, my mother would periodically sigh loudly, or say, "Oh, *please*," until I pulled her aside.

"Mom," I whispered, "there are only four of us, so paste on a fake smile right now."

She stared back at me defiantly, which put me in the strange position of having to scold her like she was an errant child. I pulled out one of her favorite expressions from my youth. "Wipe that expression off your face before I wipe it off for you," I warned.

She laughed. "Am I that obvious? Okay, I'll behave."

Back at the hotel, we consoled ourselves with slices of chocolate malt cake that were left on a silver tray in the dining room for guests.

"There were still some spooky bits," she said. "I liked when he took us to the gates of the graveyard."

I shoveled in another forkful of cake. "Well, it will make a good story for your friends at home."

But she couldn't let it rest. The next morning, before we went to the airport, we stopped by the church so she could do a little fact checking.

"Hah theyah," she said to a church lady with bouffant hair and a necklace of large fake pearls who was stationed at the door. Then she repeated the story of the thief, and the church lady laughed and told her it wasn't true.

"But I have seen a ghost right here in the church," the lady added. "That is a fact. A little girl was abducted from here years ago. She was last seen right near that pew over there." She pointed to the far side of the church. "The family was frantic. For years, I would sometimes feel her presence, but I never told Monsignor because I just felt so foolish. But then a few years ago, right after the floor had been mopped, I looked down and saw small footprints right where she had been taken. And this church was empty."

"No," breathed my mother.

The church lady nodded. "Oh, yes. Oh, yes. I will never forget seeing those little prints."

We edged closer as she told us all the details. "Now, *that* was spooky," said my mother afterward.

Then we bid that jasmine-scented city adieu and flew home to the decidedly less fragrant Newark airport. "Remind me why we live here again," I said.

"I have no idea," said my mother. "Listen, you can go ahead and take a cab to Brooklyn. I'll be fine." Of course she would. But so few opportunities arose where I could actually take care of her.

"No, I'll put you in a cab and then I'll get one," I said. We stood in line at the taxi stand. As we neared the front, I gave my mother a hug good-bye.

"This is the most vaginal weekend I've ever spent in my life," I said.

"Me, too," she replied, her eyes misting ever so slightly. Then she stepped into a cab. "Bye, baby," she drawled.

4

The Joys of a Breakfast Buffet

Every weekday morning, my best friend, Julie, drops her daughter, Violet, off at school and then calls me at precisely 9:07 as she walks to the gym in her Upper West Side neighborhood. Julie is a writer like me, so we act as makeshift co-workers for each other, having our morning chat around a symbolic watercooler.

JANCEE: How was the party last night? I hope—no, I trust—that you left early.

JULIE: Please. I was in and out in an hour and ten minutes. Home and in bed by nine.

JANCEE: I'm proud of you. (*Julie and I do not like to go out in the evening. In our entire twenty-year friendship, we have never had dinner together, as a courtesy to each other.*) Do you know what's great about getting older? Not getting looks when you say you like to go to bed early. Not getting looks when you order a seltzer instead of a vodka tonic.

JULIE: Not getting looks when you walk down the street. You know what someone said to me the other day? "If I lived near you, we would be such good friends." And I thought of that expression that you've used, from when you were a kid: "Tick-tock, the door is locked." I can't take on another friend. Unless somebody dies or moves away, then a slot opens up. Although let's be honest: If Martin Scorsese wanted to be our friend, I would have time for him. He could come to Bergdorf's with us and look at skirts. So? How was Savannah?

JANCEE: As we speak, I'm lying down with my eyes closed. Does that tell you something? But it was really fun. You were right to tell me to go. It was a little stressful to be the planner—she's used to having my father plan everything, so I had to take over. But it will be something I'll always remember. My mother won't always be so lively. You know? Now is the time.

JULIE: I want to take a trip with my mother, too. I think that it's a lot further down the road, though, when I travel for pleasure. Right now, travel means punishment to me—work, or obligatory visits. (*Lowers voice.*) Oh my God. There is a woman on the sidewalk in a heroin stupor, nodding off. She's wearing a shirt that says INSIDE THIS T-SHIRT IS ONE TERRIFIC MOM. Did she eat that mom, or snort that mom? In what case would wearing that T-shirt be a good idea anyway? I never want to wear a T-shirt that sets someone up to judge me.

So, what did you and your mom do together?

JANCEE: You know what I realized during that weekend? I've reached the age where I have the same interests as my folks. When did that happen? I like most of the things they like, with the exception of craft expos and going to Wal-Mart. But other than that, we all talk excitedly about sunblock with SPF 70 and omega-3s. As a matter of fact, I'm going to take one of those capsules right now. They're in the fridge. They're a little cloudy but I think that's okay.

JULIE: With us, it's the joys of a breakfast buffet. In our family we spend an incredible amount of time talking about what makes something in the buffet good or crappy. Like if they have fresh fruit or real granola, we're all excited. But if it's the little boxes of Kellogg's cereal, well, that's no good. If we're at a hotel and a breakfast buffet is included, it's a good thing. I could tell you my entire life of traveling based on the breakfasts of the hotel.

JANCEE: We had breakfast brought up to us on a tray in Savannah. My mother liked that, I can tell you.

JULIE: What did you eat? (*This is a very common question that we ask each other.*)

JANCEE: Biscuits and strawberry jam, fruit, muffins, and coffee.

JULIE: No protein?

JANCEE: You know what? There was protein. I forgot. We had poached eggs on a bed of grits.

JULIE: Nice. (*She is interrupted by the sound of two voices, one male and one female. When she answers them, her voice is high and warmly enthusiastic*.) Sure! Central Park? Take a left, there are three looooong blocks, and then you'll see it. There will be a lot of trees and grass. (*Aside, to me*) And maybe a used condom on the ground. Okay! Have fun! Black socks and sandals—must be German tourists. Did you ever see a famous person on the street and then you realize the person's dead?

JANCEE: Yes. I had a moment the other day when I thought I saw Norman Mailer. Why? Who did you think you saw?

JULIE: I thought I just saw Raul Julia. But then I remembered that he's not around anymore. So, what did you and your mom do together?

JANCEE: I have to say it was a little strange to spend so much concentrated time with my mother. Usually other family members are around to break it up. For the first hour it was odd, and then I got used to it.

JULIE: You know, I would like for that to happen. I really should plan something with my mother before it's too late.

JANCEE: Well, let's think here. What do the two of you like to do? What's the ultimate activity?

JULIE: (*immediately*) Outlet shopping.

JANCEE: Hold on, my cleaning lady is knocking at the door. (*Luba, my Russian cleaning lady, holds a tampon wrapper that she has retrieved from the bathroom trash can.*)

LUBA: (*sadly*) No baby?

JANCEE: No baby. Not this month, I guess.

LUBA: I pray for you to have a child.

JANCEE: Thank you. (*Luba shuts the door.*) Luba is keeping an eye on my fertility cycle, as usual. So I noticed something about my mother this weekend. She has a habit of commenting on people's appearances right in front of them. She'll say (*overly Southern, Foghorn Leghorn voice*), "Lord have mercy, look at the size of that family comin' toward us! Every one of 'em is as big as a rhino, even th' damn dawg!" In the meantime they're all standing on the same street corner as we are. You know how when you're in a foreign country you tend to speak English freely, thinking no one will understand you anyway? That's what she does, right here in America.

JULIE: My mother, if you say to her in a quiet voice, "Don't look now" or "Don't turn around," she'll say, "*What? Where?*" In the last few years she has totally lost her ability to self-edit. It's just a cringefest. She's always saying to my aunt about her daughter that when she was born she looked just like a wolf, all covered in fur. And then you'll hear my aunt say in kind of a quiet voice, "I don't remember that." But my mother isn't listening. She was just telling me about a wedding she went to, and she began with, "The bride had a good head," and then she sort of left it at that. And I knew that what was going to come next was "But the body, no good." It's never going to be "But a great body." Not with my mother.

And the other thing she told me was that a woman in her town had a bunch of kids but no teeth. Her exact words were "Many kids but no teeth."

JANCEE: I guess it's inevitable that we turn into our mothers, but I would hope we might be more tactful. But who knows? Maybe you lose that ability. Here, I'll make you feel better. How are you different from your mom?

JULIE: I think I'm a much more conscious person.

JANCEE: I don't understand.

JULIE: My mother was sort of out to lunch. I mean, she was a mother at twenty-two and I'm forty-something, and she had three kids and I have one. I live in the city and she's in the country. (*Her parents' house upstate is teeming with wildlife, so when Julie visits, she will send me emails with titles like "Hello from Snakeland."*)

But our main difference, I think, is that my mother was like a drone who went from living in her parents' house to college, and then the summer after college she met my dad and got married. She never got a chance to grow as a person. So we're very, very different in where we are in our lives when we had kids.

And she also was sort of unaware of psychology at that point. When Violet didn't want to go to pre-K, she was crying and grabbing on to my leg, and even though it was painful, I knew it was best for her to go. And my mother would have said, "Oh, she doesn't have to go." That kind of thing.

But we're the same, too, in that we march to the beat of our own drummer. I don't care what people think. When it comes to being a parent, for instance. My friend told me, "When I was at your house and I saw that Violet watched TV all the time, I thought, *My God, I would never do that.* And now I do it all the time."

JANCEE: That's heartwarming.

JULIE: Once I was doing a reading for my book, and in the audience was one of my friends, and kind of as a joke, he stood up and asked me, "What's your process?" And I said, "Turning on Noggin."

And now I'm in a mourning period because Violet doesn't watch television anymore. Let me tell you, it's hell. In the old days, she used to zone out in front of the TV. She'd lie on the couch with her blanket. I told my friend Susan, "It's like Violet always has the flu, right?"

But it's not that way anymore. Now she always wants to play. She likes going out, and being read to, and activity books and stuff. She's not very independent in her play.

JANCEE: I hear from so many parents that they aren't going to let their kids watch television, and one by one, they all cave. (*Walking into the kitchen*) You can't believe what my kitchen counter looks like. Tom obviously made breakfast before he left today. There's an open box of cereal, a bag of coffee, and a container of milk on the counter, which is now warm. You don't need to be Quincy to retrace his steps. That's how I know he'll never cheat on me, because he'd leave a trail of evidence.

JULIE: Paul is the same way. (*Paul is Julie's husband, a television producer.*) They could never commit crimes. It's that sort of inability to know the difference between mildly cleaning up and totally cleaning up. Leaving the mustard knife on the counter but putting the turkey back in the fridge.

Paul, it's not as surprising, because he doesn't seem like the most meticulous guy. Tom looks like a Felix Unger type. But he ain't! You know what? He misrepresented himself to you.

I can't decide whether to go to the grocery store or not after the gym.

JANCEE: Go home, I say. It's so humid today. Be good to yourself.

JULIE: I'm going home. It's disgusting out.

JANCEE: I'm around if you want to talk later.

JULIE: I'm sure we will.

5

Sure Are a Lot of Memories
in This Garage

I had an absurdly happy childhood growing up in the small town of Chatham, a leafy enclave in the Garden State that was more New England than New Jersey. The stores that line Main Street are out of a Capra movie: Sunnywoods Flower Shop, the Bean Curd Chinese restaurant, Helen's Dressmaking Shop, Liberty Drug (which has a working soda fountain), the Stitching Bee ("for all your needlepoint needs"). My idyllic life was to end in the early nineties when my parents announced, after much throat clearing, that they were selling our family home and moving to a lake community in northern Jersey.

My sisters and I were dumbfounded. This was our home. Granted, none of us were living there at that point, but still. My parents explained that they had remained in the house for us, but with retirement imminent, they craved a fresh start. They wanted to watch the sun set over the lake as they drank gin and tonics with their feet up.

"And to be honest, girls, we're getting a little tired of keeping up with the Joneses," said my mother, who had opted out of Chatham's country club circuit.

"So you're just going to give up and admit defeat?" said Heather. "Why not put a couch on the front porch?"

"Maybe you can use an old toilet as a planter in the front yard," I put in angrily. My father sighed wearily. "You know, the sun sets in Chatham, too. And what about seeing our friends?" Of course we were unable to see things from their point of view. We were all in floods of tears.

Despite our protestations, the house was put on the market and snapped up within a week. Before we knew it, the folks had quietly moved on an unspecified day (we informed them that we didn't want to know which one). At the time, Dinah and I lived in Hoboken, the chosen land for suburban New Jersey kids who couldn't quite commit to New York City, while Heather was finishing out her fifth (or was it sixth?) year of college in San Francisco.

At our next family get-together at the lake house, my parents presented to each of us one cardboard box with a name scribbled on the side, filled with dusty mementos. The rest of our things had been tossed.

My father, seeing our bewilderment, held up a VHS tape. "I've got a special surprise for you girls," he said. "I walked through the old house and taped a little presentation for you."

We assembled on the couch and he popped the tape into the player. It opened with a swooping shot of the garage, which was empty save for two Wiffle balls hanging by strings that my dad had stapled to the ceiling to mark where to perfectly stop the car (although he never did figure out a mechanism to discourage his teen daughters from cheerfully shearing the side-view mirrors off the Buick LeSabre, sometimes on a monthly basis).

"Here we are in the garage," my father had intoned in a somber "newscaster" voice, sounding like Walter Cronkite on the day Kennedy died. "Sure are a lot of memories in this garage."

My mother looked at my father. "I can't think of one." His stentorian narration continued. "Our first car here was a Volkswagen Bug. Got it the year we moved in. Nineteen seventy-seven. I think we also had the LeSabre, which took us from Pittsburgh to Cleveland to Chatham. That was a big, solid car. Yep, I could barely fit it in the garage! Happy times. Then your mother started working, and of course, she had to get her own LeSabre. A real beaut, two-toned. Three-toned, if you count the detail. Oh, your mother loved that car. She put two hundred thousand miles on it."

My mom interrupted him. "Jay? Are you going to reminisce about every car we've ever owned?" She grabbed the remote and hit fast-forward. Now my father was lovingly filming his workroom in the basement.

". . . girls never came down here, so it was pretty much my own place," he was saying. "I fixed a lot of hair dryers down here. Built a dollhouse or two. Why, I even built these workbenches. I hope the new people know what they're getting. A lot of—"

My mother coolly pressed fast-forward again. He was clearly going to spend a lot of time on his favorite rooms. I wondered if "his" bathroom, adjacent to the workroom, would receive a doting tribute. When the tape stopped, he was standing in Heather's bedroom. It was completely vacant. Not even the thumbtacks that held up her Howard Jones poster remained on the wall.

Heather sat up sharply. "Dad? Don't tell me that you filmed the *empty house.* Surely you have another tape of the furnished house. Right?"

He looked perplexed, his eyes darting in alarm from Heather

to Dinah to me. "Well, you already know what it looks like furnished. I thought you'd like to see it when it was empty."

Heather goggled at him. "Empty of memories? *Empty of meaning?*"

He sighed. "Do you want to see the rest of it or not?" And so we toured each bare room accompanied by Dad's commentary, which ran along of the lines of *Lotta memories here* and *Lotta hard work* and *I never did get around to replacing those baseboards.* At the end of it, he had taken the camera outside and ambushed our elderly neighbor as he was methodically collecting his mail.

"Hey, there, Paul!" my father called to him as the camera ran. "I guess we won't be meeting like this anymore." Paul eyed him suspiciously as he wrestled a catalog out of his mailbox.

"I never did get that ratchet screwdriver back that I lent you, but you know what? You go ahead and keep it," said my father heartily. "It's our last day here, and I'm making a tape for posterity. Got any words of wisdom?"

Paul hesitated, glancing around warily. "It certainly will be quieter around here without your kids," he said, not unhappily. "Best of luck to you." My father waited for more wisdom, but Paul was already making his determined plod up the driveway.

Even though we eventually grew to like the lakeside place, we still felt the inexorable pull of the old one. After a few years, Dinah was able to move on, but Heather and I simply could not. We detoured longingly past it on our way to the Short Hills mall, commenting on new developments, rejoicing in details that remained the same: the mailbox, the pachysandra bunched around the birch trees in the front yard, the tomato plants that grew on the side of the house.

We would park like stalkers across the street and, in a fog of sentimentality, reminisce about the things that none of our friends who grew up dysfunctional could believe we actually did: eating hamburgers together outside at the picnic table on summer nights spangled with fireflies, tossing a ball back and forth with our father in the yard, roller-skating in the driveway as our mother planted geraniums nearby. Of course, nostalgia had neatly obliterated the screeching and hair pulling of our hate-filled teenage years.

During that era, our parents worked constantly. My father put in six days a week at JC Penney, while my mother was a sales rep who supplied office furniture to buildings around New Jersey. Because they were so often absent, the house truly felt like it belonged to us children. We had the run of the place without the bother of payments or upkeep. The scars and marks that the house bore—the burns on the kitchen linoleum from a careless smoker at a party, the flapping screen door, loose from beer-addled teens heedlessly banging it shut—were inflicted by us girls, not by our more careful folks.

Years passed. Heather and I still drove slowly by the house. The new owners built an addition onto the dining room. Our longing grew more acute, our childhood rosier, as adult problems piled onto our shoulders. Once, when both of us were between jobs, we boldly pulled into the driveway of our old home when we saw that no one was there. "Let's pretend we still live here and we're coming home from the grocery store," I said insanely as we swung in. Then we sat for a while. Then we put the car in reverse and drove back out.

Even after we both got married and I had moved to New York City, even after Heather had decamped for small-town life in New York State, we still made biannual trips, hungrily scanning the old place. Was the makeshift tombstone for our dead Siamese cat still under the spreading oak tree near the deck? In the city, I found myself migrating from one cramped, roach-spray-scented apartment to the next—ten in total—so I romanticized the house's rolling green lawn, its luxuriously spacious laundry facilities and spare rooms decadently free of any discernible purpose (a living room *and* a den!). It was hard to get sentimental about a fifth-floor walk-up with a refrigerator that smelled like it once housed dead bodies and a super who jauntily wore his pet boa constrictor like a scarf. Heather, meanwhile, had become the mother of two rambunctious young boys she couldn't leave alone for a millisecond (the last time she did, Travis had absconded with her nail polish and neatly lacquered his baby brother's eyebrows so that he resembled a shiny ventriloquist's dummy).

One September afternoon as we staked out the old house, I could stand it no longer. "I've got to see the inside," I said. "This is unsatisfying. How can we get in?"

Heather thought for a moment. "I've got it," she said finally. Travis had recently turned three, and Halloween was a month away. "We could take him trick-or-treating in this neighborhood and say that he has to use the bathroom," she said excitedly. "Actually, he always does have to use the bathroom. Or I could have him pretend to choke on a piece of candy and we could ask for a glass of water. Then we're in."

I grabbed her shoulders, moved that she would train her young son to fake a hazardous accident. "Perfect," I whispered.

And so the following month, we plucked a confused Travis from his own neighborhood in New York State, where he fully expected to go trick-or-treating with his pals, dressed him in a Peter Pan costume, and drove him an hour and a half to the Jersey neighborhood where we grew up and he did not. It was a little unnerving to carry a child across state lines for my own purposes, but I reasoned that the end result for Travis would be a big pile of candy either way, so what was the difference, really?

"I'm hungry, Mommy," he said as we headed into the neighborhood.

Heather winced. "Oh, God. In all the excitement, I think I forgot to feed him dinner. Maybe one of these houses will offer nuts, or an apple or something."

I turned around. "We'll get you some nuts, okay?"

He frowned. "Nuggets?"

I looked at Heather helplessly, and she said, "No, honey, not chicken nuggets. Nuts! Some nice, fun nuts!"

We parked the car a few streets over from our target. It was just starting to grow dark, and packs of costumed kids—princesses and superheroes and more princesses and more superheroes—were already roaming the neighborhood.

"Every single boy is a superhero," I said. "We should have dressed him as Spider-Man. Then he could have gone back to the houses multiple times and gotten more candy."

Heather looked across the street at a hulking black SUV idling at the curb. "Tell me they're not going to drive the kids to the next house," she said as three costumed children ran back to the SUV and climbed in. It moved forward three yards and then the kids got out again.

We started a couple of houses down the street to warm Travis up. "Okay, Travis," I chirped. "Now the fun begins! Go on up to the house, and don't forget that your Aunt Jancee likes peanut butter cups, so if you see them, grab two." I gave him a gentle shove.

He looked around, puzzled. "Where am I?"

"You're in Candy Land!" I said brightly. He didn't buy it.

"This is where I used to trick-or-treat when I was a kid," said Heather. "We thought you would like it."

Travis walked slowly up the stairs of a newly built McMansion that loomed over a tiny strip of decimated yard. We trailed protectively behind him, curious to see the interiors of some of these behemoths. Who lived there?

The door flew open and a well-coiffed yoga mom stood with a silver tray that held a variety of full-sized candy bars, which elicited an involuntary pang of greed in me.

"Aren't you adorable," she said as Travis's "Trick or treat" echoed in the cavernous hall behind her. We could glimpse a few pieces of furniture pushed against the wall as if they were in a police lineup. They looked puny against the hallway's cathedral ceiling.

On we went. As Travis walked to the next house, he passed a large stuffed scarecrow that lounged on a bench in the front yard. Suddenly with a yowl it sprang gruesomely to life, and Travis gave a dog-whistle scream and tearfully ran for Heather. As he clung to her legs and sobbed, I reacted with the empathy of the childless. *Faker,* I thought.

The scarecrow sheepishly approached us. "Sorry, buddy," he said to Travis. "Didn't mean to scare you that bad." He took off his tattered hat. "See? I'm just a regular guy."

"Come on, Travis," I said. "Do you know any scarecrows with goatees? No, you do not."

"I want to go back to the car," Travis whimpered. Even at the age of three, the poor child already had a history of being exploited by his aunt. When he was a baby, I loved to make surrealist films of him. I'd lodge his nice, round head in a bowl of fruit, for instance. He was such a sweet-natured little fellow that it never seemed to bother him when I dressed him in a tiny tank top and gold chain and had him act out a *Sopranos* episode for the camera.

Gamely he dried his tears, and Heather and I led him to our old house. I rang the doorbell with my heart thumping. A smiling teenage girl answered. "Hi, Peter Pan," she said to Travis as

Heather and I craned our necks past her to see the flowered wallpaper they had put up in the hallway.

After Travis took some candy out of her basket, Heather nudged him to mime the choking scene they had carefully rehearsed, but he'd fallen into a hypnotic trance at the sight of a full-sized Snickers. I looked at Heather and telegraphed, *Ask to use the bathroom.*

You do it, she telegraphed back.

No, you, I signaled.

You!

Do it! I'm older and I command you!

But you can talk your way into anything! Remember when you convinced that IRS agent not to audit you?

Hm. You might be right. I sent him a card afterward that said "I love the IRS." Remember? He hung it in his office. Mr. Shelborne, I think his name was. He was a great guy.

Good. So you know what to do. Just tell her you have—

The door clicked shut.

Travis looked pleadingly at Heather. "Can we go home now?"

Defeated, we trudged back to the car. "We have to stop," said Heather. "We just have to stop this."

We didn't bring it up again. I thought that perhaps we were finally cured, until two months later, when I received a dizzying email, written by a woman who had read my memoir and realized that she was living in our former house. Would I like to come and see it?

I couldn't breathe.

Her family would be moving to Italy soon, she continued, but before they left, they'd be happy to show me around.

I excitedly phoned Heather, who phoned Dinah, who phoned my parents.

The woman and I arranged for a tour for the following Tuesday. I asked if I might bring a family member or two, skimming over the fact that every one of us had enthusiastically signed up to attend.

On the big day, we all met in a nearby park. My parents had brought two enormous boxes of doughnuts and cups of coffee for our hosts. We were all twitching with excitement, even my toddler niece and nephew.

As the whole crew trooped up the walkway, I grabbed Heather's arm and squeezed it. "I feel sick," she whispered.

We assembled on the porch and rang the doorbell. The door opened to reveal a pretty, smiling brunette and a teenage boy and girl. "Come on in!" the mother said grandly.

We were in. We were in! I did a quick scan. The living room was intact, and looked brighter. I was used to my folks' gloomy but easy-care brown wall-to-wall and stain-hiding dark-patterned couches. The light was disorienting without the familiar sun-blotting beige drapes my parents favored, hung over sheer curtains that caught any escaping rays so that our living room remained lodged in a perpetual Norwegian winter, no matter what the season.

Heather saw my confused face. "Look at the fireplace," she prompted quietly. It had the same mantel, at least. We smiled at each other.

"Isn't this pretty," said my mother. All of us stared at the living room. Even the teens looked at it with mild interest, as if they were seeing it for the first time.

Mercifully, my father broke the silence. "Is there a place to put these doughnuts down?" he asked. "You don't need to tell me where the kitchen is."

Clutching one another as if we were entering a mine, we all

made our way through the hall. Were we really going to have doughnuts and coffee in our old kitchen? They probably had stripped the walls of the drab oak cabinets and tan plaid wallpaper, but surely the kitchen table was in the same spot. There was nowhere else to put it, really. And of course the pantry had to be in the right-hand corner.

We stepped into an enormous white room and looked around, disoriented. The kitchen had been gutted and expanded to twice the size, the ceiling raised to a dizzying height. A huge island took the place of our table. We took in the designer refrigerator and stove, the wall of untouched cookbooks.

"Look at all those new windows," said Dinah after a minute. She smiled at the teens. "I bet you guys have to clean these, don't you?" They laughed and said no.

I followed my father's gaze and saw that he was looking beyond the wall of windows to the yard. The deck that he had built had been torn down, replaced by the kitchen addition. "Wow, I never realized we were so close to the neighbors," he said.

Dinah joined him and looked out the windows. "No, you see, Dad? The neighbors put on an addition, too."

He nodded. "Oh. Right," he said absently.

We gathered around the kitchen island and made small talk, asking the teens about their teachers. They lost their shyness and regaled us with funny stories as we microwaved the coffee, which had grown lukewarm, and ate the doughnuts. Then the kids, now outgoing, volunteered to show us their rooms. I heard Heather's sharp intake of breath when she saw the way that her old bedroom, once bright yellow and frilly, had been transformed by the boy into a dank lair, strewn with the usual teen-boy detritus. My bedroom, meanwhile, was unrecognizable with its gleaming new floors and spiffy wall paneling. I quickly took it all in, trying to appear discreet even as my head joggled around like a cat following a fly. I hoped so much to discover an artifact, even a small one, from the years spent dreaming on my bed and writing in my diary. Nothing. Even the baseboards had been replaced.

Our tour ended with a peek into the master bedroom, but we felt hesitant to barge in, especially after the owner had been so accommodating.

"Well, thanks so much for doing this," I ventured as we walked down the stairs to the hallway. I didn't meet Heather's eyes, but I knew her thoughts mirrored mine. What had we been craving, exactly, with this little excursion?

I suppose I had wanted to spot something wonderfully mundane—homely, even—that would instantly transport me through an emotional time machine. If we were standing inside of a kitchen that we recognized, surrounded by all of our family members—still alive, still miraculously healthy—then we could achieve the impossible and actually go home again. But there was not a familiar relic to be found, not a doorknob, not a light switch. And really, who could blame the woman for tossing out the funereal linoleum, the gruesome light-blue toilet in my father's "special" bathroom that the rest of us only used in direst emergency? Our house had been a symphony of browns—not tasteful chocolate brown, either, but dingy grime-brown, built to capably hide the filth generated by a thousand kids trooping in and out. Hell, I would have swept through the place like Hannibal's army.

Still. My chest hitched a little and I dared not meet Heather's eyes.

"Oh, girls," said the woman suddenly. "I almost forgot. Stay there." She ran upstairs to the attic, and we heard her scavenging around. Then she bounded down the stairs, clutching a furry object.

"This is a little piece of your old bedroom rug," she said to me. "I saved it. I can remember visiting my old house after I grew up, and I thought I'd keep it just in case the old owners came by."

She handed the little square to me. It was my old-fashioned hooked rug, with a black background and a cream-and-pink floral design that I used to trace with my fingers as I lay on the floor and listened to records. Heather reached out and gingerly petted it.

"Thank you," I said feelingly.

The woman laughed. "I have one more thing to show you." She led us into her bedroom and opened her bathroom door. "I didn't renovate this one," she said. "I figured that no one would see it but me, so why bother, right? Feel free to stay in here and look around. I should probably go down and join your parents."

The bathroom was exactly the same: the blue tiles, the laundry chute, the ancient fixtures. Hysterical laughter bubbled up in both of us as at the same time we spotted the mirrored toothbrush holder that swung discreetly back into the wall, a relic from our childhood that was dated even back then.

"It's as crusty and tacky as ever!" Heather said with a gasp. "Look, there's some toothpaste stains. They could even be ours! I've never been so glad to see something in my life."

"Me, too," I said. "And look at the shower door! The handle is still wobbly." We stayed in that bathroom for a full ten minutes, trying to get ourselves together, and then a wave of cackling would overtake us again.

"I wonder where the girls are?" I heard my mother say downstairs.

Heather drew herself up and smoothed her hair. "We've been up here too long," she said. "Let's go. Come on." She grabbed my shoulders. "Wait a minute," she said suddenly. "It's over, right?"

64 • Jancee Dunn

I nodded. Of course, we couldn't really go home again. Our folks had aged. Hell, Heather and I had aged. One week earlier, we had been comparing spider-vein patterns on our legs.

"It's over," I said. Clutching my ratty square of carpet, I followed her down the stairs.

6

Salty, Sweet, Gritty Blobs of Joy

My friend Lou was once my producer when I was a veejay on MTV2, MTV's sister channel. During the inexplicable five years that I was on the air (I was the most ramblingly unprofessional television personality in the history of Viacom), Lou and I found that we shared a number of interests, including schlocky movies and sugary foods. Lou soon got into the habit of leaving meandering messages on my answering machine rhapsodizing about his latest food discovery. He often gets so swept up that he must leave his message in two parts. For instance:

> Hi, it's Lou. Okay, so my current obsession is Baskin-Robbins chocolate chip cookie dough ice cream—first of all, because there are lots of chunks. There's not random pieces like, "Look, there's one up ahead"—they're all over the place. And the vanilla ice cream, while probably extremely artificial, is so appealingly, blindingly, *Clorox-bleach*

white, it's like a dream, and then you have these salty, sweet, gritty blobs of joy. And the more you eat—obviously out of the container because it tastes best out of the container— the more the snow melts, and it becomes this delicious thick, cold soup with chunky surprises, and you keep digging into the mountain like a treasure hunt to find more. There's so much joy in that half-gallon!

So it says on the container that there are only eleven grams of fat per serving, and I don't know what's happening to me that I suddenly think eleven grams a serving is okay. And I don't know how many servings there are in a half-gallon. My belief is that there would be four, but it's probably in the double digits. And the only reason I got the ice cream is because I worked out really hard today at the gym so I wanted to ruin whatever progress I made by going to get a Reese's Whipps. Have you ever had a Whipp? It's like a 3 Musketeers, except the nougat is peanut butter.

Anyway, I was walking home with my Whipp in my pocket, and in the distance, I see the welcoming fluorescent white-and-pink colors of the Dunkin' Donuts and Baskin-Robbins combo store that's open 24-7. So I go in, just to check inventory. I thought, *They probably don't even have the cookie dough.* [*beep*]

Lou again. What the hell is with your machine? Anyway, they had it, so I felt it was a sign I should buy it. And the lid of the container was even ripped.

Me, aloud to the machine: "What, with the dirt that could get in, or mold? Microbes? Insect legs? I would never have bought it."

You would never have bought it, but I did anyway. I had to. Why I needed that half-gallon in my house, I don't know. I thought, *Lou, when you get home, don't do what you did last time, which is eat almost all of it. When you get home, have the Whipp, put the ice cream in the freezer, and enjoy it another night. Eat the Whipp, then have an apple, and then thirty-two ounces of water or something.*

So I came in, took my shoes off, and immediately opened the ice cream and began eating it. I didn't even hesitate. It was like I never even had that thought. Later I thought, *Water, apple—what?* So I ate probably three quarters of the container. I think my eyes were dilated at this point. And so that I wouldn't eat the rest, I sprayed Caldrea Green Tea Patchouli Countertop Cleanser on it, which happened to be nearby.

And then, a half hour later, I ate the Whipp. [*beep*]

If I'm not receiving phone messages, I'm being sent emails with semi-pornographic subject lines like *Mmmm* or *Oh My God* or *I'd Eat This for Sure* and underneath, a link to some obscure food purveyor Lou has unearthed: a Maine-based vendor of whoopie pies ("I'd get the one with peanut butter filling, or maybe raspberry") or a bakery in north Jersey that sells tiramisu-flavored cakes.

So when either of us is feeling down, we cheer ourselves up with a long-standing ritual: We meet at a grocery store, load up the cart, and then proceed to Lou's apartment, where we camp out on the couch and have ourselves a Lifetime-movie film festival. Lou lives in Gramercy Park, and his building is one of the few that actually overlooks the park itself, a beautifully manicured refuge and one of only two private parks in New York City (the other is in Queens). Lou has a coveted key to the park, but does he ever go in there? No. He prefers to stay indoors. "It's hardly a park, anyway," he sniffs. "It's like a little patch of land with a fence around it. It's not like there are rides or anything."

I phoned him one recent Saturday morning. "No one calls me anymore," I said. This was true. Most of my friends communicated via email, so that depending on my mood, my apartment could seem peaceful or mausoleum quiet. On this particular day, I felt like Omega Man as I pictured bustling homes in the city where the phone jingled merrily all day. Although if mine rang all the time, I'd be irritable. *God, I'm tedious,* I thought, and picked up the phone.

"I think I need to get out of my apartment," I told him.

"Meet me at Whole Foods," said Lou. "I'll need about two hours to get going." Lou always required long lead times before meeting me, although it was unclear what he actually did during them. He usually mumbled something about getting wrapped up in some Internet search (his latest being Whatever happened to Joyce Hyser from *Just One of the Guys* and Deborah Foreman from *Valley Girl*?)

We used to start our ritual at a regular grocery store near Lou's apartment before we discovered the giant, gleaming Whole Foods on the Bowery downtown, the high temple of twelve-dollar salad dressing often referred to as "Whole Paycheck." The place filled me with equal parts giddiness and shame, with its temperature-controlled walk-in cheese cave, the Beer Room with two hundred different brews, the thin-crust pizza bar, the Pommes Frites counter with twelve varieties of dipping sauces, the gelato bar with irritatingly seductive flavors like black mission fig and crème fraîche. The Bowery had changed profoundly from its skid row past of the sixties and seventies, when down-and-outers would weave in and out of the fetid flophouses that lined the streets (many with incongruously upbeat names like the Dandy and the Palace). Now the area was studded with sleek multimillion-dollar lofts and peopled with trust-fund kids and starlets who weaved in and out of pricey bars.

Lou met me at the door of Whole Foods, announcing briskly that we had plenty of ground to cover. He liked to inspect virtually every product in the store. We started in the cheese section, where he snatched up a container. "You can't go wrong with pimento cheese spread."

"No, you cannot." I tossed it into our basket.

He wasn't listening because he was homing in on a package of flatbreads. "Flatbreads for $14.99?" he said, frowning. "What the hell is in them?" He threw it down. "Ooh, samples! Mm, rosemary crostini." He popped one in his mouth.

"I can't believe you would eat something sitting out for public consumption," I said with a shudder.

"Get over it." He brightened. "Look, they have *burrata*."

"What's that?"

"It's like a thin pouch of mozzarella filled with cheese and cream. God, it's so delicious. If you were Italian, you'd be genuflecting right now, trust me." His eyes roamed sharply over the shelves. "Blue-cheese dip, bring it on. I would eat that entire container. Cheddar cheese spread with port wine. I mean, there's no wrong time." A tattooed girl with platinum hair reached around Lou to get some artichoke dip, and he gave her a black look. "What's with the pushing and shoving?" he said. She moved away, unconcerned.

"Yes, but you were just standing there," I said. "She was actually buying something."

"Still, she didn't have to be rude. God, I hate everyone." *Uh-oh.* Lou's mood could plunge if he started his harangue about the culture's decline in civility. More than once, he had fumed through an entire movie because a patron did not move his feet as we struggled past him to a pair of empty seats. I had to distract him.

"Look, a new product," I said, pointing to a tasteful pyramid of cracker packages.

He ran over. "Ooh! Raincoast Crisps!"

I shook my head. "You don't even know what that is, so why are you excited?"

As Lou perused the shelves, he also browsed some of the male customers. "Red shirt," he said quietly. A husky guy with an open, friendly face was picking up a package of chicken franks.

"He's cute," I agreed. Lou's preferences ran to what he called "jamokes"—big, clean-cut guys. "I like regular Joes," he said. "Unfortunately for me, they're usually not gay." Lou, whom any Italian grandmother would call "a nice-looking boy," had a touch of the jamoke himself, preferring to wear baggy plaid shirts, jeans, and running shoes.

We inspected the dessert bar, with its troughs of bread pudding and apple crisp, then moved on to cookies and candy. "Nothing's screaming 'Eat me,'" Lou said. He held up a pack of cookies. "Although I do like anything with the word *crème* on it. It has to be spelled that way because then you know it's junky and good." He moved to return the package and was blocked by a chiseled man who was clearly a model. "I love the way he puts his carriage in the middle of the aisle!" Lou barked as I hustled him away.

An hour and a half later we were lugging our bags into Lou's apartment, a dark, comfortable cavern with honey-colored Mission furniture and a giant couch with a slight but unmistakable butt-shaped indentation situated on the right side. He closed the living room curtains to block out every particle of the cheery afternoon sun, swept aside the teetering pile of entertainment magazines on the coffee table, and we set out our repast.

"And now," Lou announced, producing a custom DVD folder from a nearby shelf, "what to watch?" With a frown of concentration, he flipped through the pages, stuffed with dozens of Louvies, his term for his beloved Lifetime and made-for-TV "films" starring television stalwarts like Judith Light and Valerie Bertinelli as women in peril. The golden age of Lou-vies—and certainly some Lifetime film scholars will debate this—was approximately 1979 to 1996. A few constants tied them together: The lead actresses were thrown into grave danger of some kind; the movies were inevitably shot in Toronto, which stood in as a sort of Everycity; and any actor of color was usually consigned to the role of sympathetic cop or concerned caseworker.

In the late nineties, some progress was made when the lead actress would have a skeptical black friend who just had a *bad feeling* about her pal's new boyfriend and was thus able to graduate to slightly meatier lines such as "Courtney, what do you really know about him?" and "I just think you're moving too fast, that's all" before she is last heard on an answering machine: "Courtney, I'm going through Cole's desk. Seems like you don't know everything about this guy. It turns out he k— (*gasping and strangling sounds*)."

"Hm," Lou said absently. "Maybe we should watch *Maid of Honor,* with Linda Purl, where she's crazy in love with her brother-in-law? Her sister dies and she moves in to take care of the family, and wants to be the new wife. But the guy gets a girlfriend. As it happens, the new girlfriend is allergic to peanuts, so Linda secretly feeds her peanuts by mixing them into a recipe. Classic."

"I saw that one already with you last year. Remember?"

He flipped past *Sins of the Mind, The Horror at 37,000 Feet,* and *Touched by Evil.* "Okay, what about this one, one of my all-time favorites, called *Who Will Love My Children?*"

I nodded. "Keep talking."

"Dying farm woman, played by Ann-Margret, has to give away her thirty-seven kids. And her farmer husband is a drunk, played by Fred Ward. Or maybe it was Frederic Forrest."

"That sounds too dark," I said doubtfully.

"Whatever. *See Jane Run*—oh, I loved that one. Starring

Joanna Kerns, who finds herself wandering through a supermarket wearing a trench coat, and underneath, she's covered in blood. Or maybe *A Time to Live,* starring Liza Minnelli, and Corey Haim as her dying son. Absolutely hilarious." He flipped another page. "Oooh! *Lady Killer* with Judith Light and Jack Wagner. That could be good. Bored rich housewife has an affair with Jack Wagner, who turns out to be insane. He ends up shtupping her daughter, played by Tracey Gold."

I considered it. "That seems more upbeat, but somehow it's still not quite right."

"Picky. Let me think. I know! Let's do a Tori Spelling film festival. We can start with *Housesitter,* where she takes care of a house and meets some gardener, and it turns out that her husband is really a piece of shit. I think."

"Lou, what are you talking about? Whose husband? What gardener? That sounds like a disjointed plot, even for Lifetime."

"I actually don't remember, I'll have to watch again. Ah. Here's a classic, *Mother, May I Sleep with Danger?* Tori's a track-star overachiever who falls in love with some guy who turns out to be an abusive, possessive boyfriend. And we need to watch *Co-ed Call Girl,* definitely. She's this studious girl who becomes an escort when someone plays a practical joke on her or something. At first she thinks she's going to be an escort, like a regular escort that goes to parties as a date, as if that even exists. Then she finds out it involves blow jobs."

"Done."

He put in *Mother, May I Sleep with Danger?* and lowered himself into his butt-shaped indentation while I took the left side of the couch and loaded some artichoke dip onto a cracker. As we watched Tori go through the motions of being a bookworm, Lou suddenly heaved a gloomy sigh.

I looked over at him. "What? Is this not funny enough?" We were permitted to chat if there were no high-drama scenes taking place on-screen.

"No, it's not that. This dip is just not cheering me up the way I thought it would. I saw my parents last weekend, and I don't know, I just can't shake this depression." Lou often visited his folks in Hoboken, New Jersey, where his father was born and raised. His mother had come to America from Molfetta, Italy, when she was fourteen. They met when they were both working in a ladies' coat factory. Now in their seventies, they still lived in the brownstone where they had raised Lou and his two siblings.

The habitual banter between Lou and me had taken a somber turn in the past year as his father weathered kidney trouble. During a series of late-night phone conversations we tried to contemplate a future without our parents, but for the most part our imaginations—usually a little too florid—failed us completely. It was inconceivable, even as it happened to people we knew and we witnessed their sadness and blind shock, even as I found myself, more and more, making tactful corrections when I talked to friends such as "Are you spending Thanksgiving with your par— with your mother?" I remember, years ago, seeing a co-worker return to the office two weeks after her mother had died of cancer and being shocked. How could she walk and talk?

So Lou and I cautiously tried to discuss it, thinking that with a frank conversation, somehow we could prepare ourselves mentally for the day that our parents would not be there, but after many attempts we were no closer to acceptance. I would watch my folks as they talked about the death of their own parents and see the bewilderment creep onto their faces, decades later. I noticed the almost imperceptible hesitation when my mother would say, "When Mama . . . died . . ." and knew that saying the word *died* would never, ever come naturally. As my parents reminisced, the years fell away and they looked like wistful children, and it was then that I knew there was no real preparing.

"What happened?" I asked him, alarmed. "Did your dad have a health setback?"

"No, it's just more of a general realization. They've gotten older and it's difficult to watch. The roles are shifting a little. You understand their need for you as opposed to it always being about you needing them. And it's not because they're telling you but because you're seeing it, you're feeling it." He sighed and reached for a Raincoast Crisp.

"And I want to be there for them, after everything they've done for me. Which they did joyously. They really wanted me around, enjoyed giving me food off of their plate." He snorted. "Which I would never do. Eat your own! And I really don't think it was a front. I like kids, but from a distance. I just don't have the patience."

"I don't know how people do it," I said. "And unfortunately for me, my favorite things to do require a calm atmosphere. My idea of a perfect afternoon is reading a book from cover to cover without anyone bothering me."

"Right. If I had a kid, I would constantly be like, 'Leave me alone, I want to watch *Lost*.' But you know, both my parents were working-class—my father started out doing construction, my mother was a seamstress. So you can't think of them like parents today. There were no playdates, no 'Mommy and Me.' It was a blue-collar upbringing. I was disciplined, and there was yelling and the occasional spank. But I do *not* wake up screaming because of it."

I nodded. "I was spanked, too. It's hard to think of my folks that way now, because their personalities have softened so much."

"Mine, too. My father used to be a sterner man. Now he's a lot more gentle. And I can't even remember when it started, but now my mother is saying 'I love you' a lot. You know, at first it was kind of weird. Even though Italians are stereotypically demonstrative and emotional, it's sort of a bullshit cliché. We can be just as WASPy, in the sense that there are not a lot of intimate conversations about the subtlety of feelings. It's black and white. It's either 'I'm very angry!' or 'I'm full of love!'"

He dipped a Mucho Nacho baked tortilla chip—our "healthy" snack—into a jar of queso blanco cheese dip. "But I've gotten used to it and now I say it right back. Although it makes me hyperventilate because I think it's a sign of my mother coming to terms with her mortality."

I just let Lou talk, while I inwardly adjusted to seeing him so vulnerable. He was easily my most caustic friend, but he always argued that if you scratch a cynic, you'll discover a disappointed idealist.

I told him that I had begun to give my parents little gifts, and to quietly pick up the tab for various excursions, despite their discomfort in accepting it.

"My mother's always giving me coffee money," said Lou. "I'm always like, 'Ma, I don't drink that much coffee.' And my father is constantly asking me, 'Is there anything you need?'"

I loaded some port wine cheese onto a cracker and absently watched Tori screaming and running down a dock. I've always had a soft spot for Tori, whom I had once interviewed for *Harper's Bazaar.* She was no Phi Beta Kappa, but so sweetly friendly, so game to my request to open her purse and show me what was inside (Child perfume, a strawberry Lip Smacker). During our lunch at Cravings in Los Angeles, she vowed never to do another cheesy TV movie. Tori did not yet understand how much comfort and pleasure her Lifetime legacy would bring to thousands— millions, even.

I gently returned to the subject of Lou's father. Lou sighed again and told me his health was stable, but not what it had been. "Look, they're both in their seventies, and my obvious fear is losing them. There's an obsession with death among Italians." He imitated his mother, somber. "'Lou, *guess who died.* My nephew's cousin's best friend—you met him at Vito's confirmation.'" He shook his head. "They're always going to a wake, the way some people go to sporting events. Where I grew up, death was discussed, but when it comes to my parents . . ." He trailed off. "If I lose them—"

"I like that you say *if,*" I broke in.

"You never know. I could go first. That would be horrible for them. And for me, depending on how." I looked at his face and could see that he was imagining gruesome TV-movie-style ways to die—being trapped in a burning car that sails over a cliff, falling from the roof of an abandoned warehouse while being pursued by an obsessed ex-husband played by Richard Grieco. He shook himself out of it. "As you get older," he went on, "your parents ultimately become the best, most loyal friends you've ever had. And then you have to think about losing them." He scowled. "Which is annoying."

I scraped up the last of the artichoke dip. "And the irony is that when you get older, your world gets smaller," I added. "When I was in my twenties, a close friend was any girl who held my hair back as I threw up my eighth Jell-O shot. Now that I'm older, I don't have room for friendships that aren't real."

"And at our age, it's just so easy for people to vanish," he said.

We both stared, unseeing, at the television screen.

"Not that I'm playing the violin, but after losing my parents, it will just be me, alone in my apartment," Lou continued. "My sister will be there, but she has two kids and a husband."

I looked over at him, and his stricken expression was too much for me. I needed to see a glimpse of the Artist Formerly Known as Lou.

"Stop it," I snapped. "You act like you're some sort of friendless, forgotten octogenarian, parked away in some nursing home. You've got a million people around you. And having a mate, or kids, does not automatically inoculate you against loneliness."

He shrugged, the classic Italian *What are you gonna do* gesture. "Yeah, but you and I both know it's not quite the same thing as being single."

We sat for a while in silence as Tori bashed her abusive boyfriend's head in with an oar.

Lou heaved himself up. "I'm so bloated," he announced. "Well, should I put in *Co-ed Call Girl*?"

I reached for an oatmeal chocolate chip cookie. "You know what? I think I'm bloated from too much Tori. Maybe we need something lighter. If that's possible."

Lou consulted his DVD collection. "How about *Face of Evil*? Tracey Gold murders a girl in an airport bathroom and assumes her identity at art school, where she ends up getting it on with her dorm-mate's father, played by Perry King."

I settled back on the couch. "Perfect."

7

You Can't Go Wrong
with Puppies

Julie makes her usual phone call to me en route to the gym. On this particular morning, she has just dropped her daughter, Violet, off at a new school. Violet has recently transferred there.

JULIE: My kid told me something yesterday that no parent wants to hear. She said, "I don't want to go to that school anymore. The kids in the class don't like me."

JANCEE: Oh, Lord. She's been there, what, three weeks?

JULIE: And I said, "Wh-what?" So today I talked to the teacher at drop-off, and she said, "I don't know why they wouldn't like her." Then she remembered that Violet tried to sit down with some girls in the cafeteria, and they pushed her away from the table. But the thing Violet told me had to do with another incident. A kid told her she was mean because she was playing with the Magna-Tiles wrong.

JANCEE: What are Magna-Tiles? I'm not familiar with kid items.

JULIE: They're these magnetic plastic tiles and you can build things. I'm not quite clear how she was playing wrong in a mean way, and it's also not like her, because she shares everything. And as a parent, what you find yourself doing when you hear this is that you want to tell her why each of these kids is inferior. "Well, that girl has very thin, mousy hair, and it's not easy for her to see the goodness in people."

JANCEE: Well, good for you for taking action and going to the teacher.

JULIE: Please, I'm so on top of this. But of course the other thing I always think is, *What's the thing I'm going to do that's going to put Violet in therapy?* I just picture her saying, "Mom, why didn't you just *back off*? Everything that happened to me, you had to run and talk to the teacher." And the truth is that at this age, they do forget and move on. At five, they're not in the grudge years yet. So I know that tomorrow she's probably not going to come in and have the same thing happen.

JANCEE: That makes sense. But I can absolutely remember that sick-making feeling of being frozen out. Can't you? Although I must say, it takes a while to call up those feelings because I've tamped them down so thoroughly over the years. You spend your entire adulthood trying to forget them.

JULIE: Oh, sure. And now I think, *How do I arm my kid?* The best thing to do is to make sure they have a strong-enough sense of self that they can get through these things. Because that's life, and the best way is to be able to be tough enough to stand up to that kind of thing. If you can do that, you can do anything. I mean, before eight hundred years of therapy, I was the kind of person who, if anybody would look at me funny, I would get a stomachache and think, *What can I do to fix this? Should I buy them a present, maybe?*

JANCEE: When I was younger I was bullied by a couple of girls, but my mother would never have dreamed of going to the teacher or a kid's mom. They just didn't do that stuff then. It was before the awareness of bullying and all the *20/20* specials about it. It was a more oblivious time in general. I used to sit in the front seat of the car when my mother would drive, and she'd smoke with her left hand so her right arm would be free to reach over and hold me back if we made a sudden stop. Anyway, I vividly remember that when I got bullied I wanted her to step in somehow, but I wonder now if that would have made things worse for me.

JULIE: I think there has got to be a way that parents can get in there. There is a way. I do believe that children can't rule the world, and sometimes it takes a parent stepping in and asking their kid how they would feel if they were treated that way.

(*Disembodied voice*) Can somebody take me across the street?

I have to hang up. (*A minute later*) Okay, me again. I had to help a blind man across the street. (*Julie regularly helps blind people across the street.*) Of course, as I did that, the light was about to turn and we had to really run. I practically dragged him. He was probably safer without me.

Anyway, what were we talking about?

JANCEE: Being harassed in school. I would imagine it's hard as a parent to find those magic words of comfort. When I would get upset after getting pushed around, my mom would say, "I know it's hard for you to understand, but someday when you're older, none of this will matter." But when you're a kid, you can't think beyond next week. At that age, the future is this alien concept where you're driving around in an aerocar like George Jetson.

JULIE: My mother probably said similar things to me, but I was so sure that no one anywhere could possibly understand or help me with those problems. So I'm always aware of that, I'm always asking Violet, "What's going on?" Really, with this situation, what I have to say is, "You don't need everybody to be your friend. You already have friends. Focus on them and not those other people."

JANCEE: That's perfect.

JULIE: But you're right, those feelings can come right back to you. When I first went to Violet's new school, and I felt as though the parents were a little "Oh, *hi*," I was like, "*Don't you fuck with me! I am better than any of you!* I'm Clint Eastwood and Tina Turner!" It makes me so angry when anybody acts exclusive to me. Anyway, I'm going to crack this nut, and I'm not sure how yet.

JANCEE: Hm. What could you do?

JULIE: A couple of playdates are a good thing. Maybe bring our two puppies in to school. In Violet's old school when I brought our dog Beatrice, the kids would go crazy.

JANCEE: You can't go wrong with puppies.

JULIE: Anyway, like you I remember that awful feeling so clearly that for the briefest moment, it made me hesitate about having kids. Because you know they're going to experience what you experienced. Kids are so unbelievably cruel.

JANCEE: And I've been on the other side of that, too. I've been nasty plenty of times myself, just flat-out mean in the most scarily creative, subversive way. But I didn't know you ever hesitated about having kids. I, on the other hand, just fell into yet another conversation with someone who tried to convert me to motherhood.

JULIE: Again with that?

JANCEE: (*sighs*) Remember that dinner party I went to on Saturday? For the entire night, Beth's husband harangued me about it. For whatever reason, I get a lot of men who try to talk me into it. I know people mean well, but I'm so tired of feeling like a sociopath when I tell them I'm on the fence.

JULIE: What's your percentage these days of being for it versus against?

JANCEE: I'm fifty-fifty. I swear to God. Not even fifty-one–forty-nine. And so is Tom. We spend so much time talking about it we could both scream. Like last weekend, aside from the dinner party, which started at eight—

JULIE: Eight P.M.? What are we, in Spain? (*Julie and I, as I have mentioned, enjoy a distinctly senior-citizen lifestyle that includes eating early and going to bed soon after that.*)

JANCEE: Tom and I just had the best time. We pick up and just go. We went out to breakfast, to the Met, to the park. I read three books.

JULIE: Now, that is a luxury, I will say.

JANCEE: On Sunday we made a big dinner and planned a trip to Budapest. I just keep thinking, *Why mess with this?* But then again, I suppose I can take a kid to breakfast and the park.

JULIE: Well, you're off birth control. Maybe something will happen, still.

JANCEE: But you know what, Jul? Forty has come and gone. I just don't think it's in the cards for me. And I'm okay with it. It just seems like no one else is okay with it.

JULIE: So quit worrying about what everyone else thinks.

JANCEE: And the thing is that— (*disembodied voice*) Oh, thank you.

That was Tom, bringing me a cup of tea with lemon. That's another thing: It's not just the freedom we have to do what we like. It's that I finally found this person, after decades of searching.

You and I have talked about that. We both got married in our thirties.

JULIE: Which I think was smart.

JANCEE: And I'm so relieved to have met him that we really treat each other well. I'm right where I want to be, and I'm fulfilled. (*Getting a little teary*) And I see couples who have a baby and they're exhausted and snap at each other and I just don't know if I want to strain my marriage. You know? In a way, I feel like I just met him.

JULIE: What is making you so upset? Beth's husband? He's an idiot. Listen, I know people who are very happy about the fact that they didn't end up having kids, and their lives are perfectly complete. For sure it's not for everybody. And it's something that so many people do automatically because it's what you do, and the idea of being thoughtful about it, thinking about it, deciding if it's the right thing to do, is such an incredibly conscious move that most people don't make. And there is not enough affirmation of that choice. I really do believe that. And there are people about whom I say, "It's great that they didn't have kids." And I mean that not in a condemning way, but in a supportive way.

JANCEE: (*sniffling*) Thank you. I believe it.

JULIE: You know I've told you that you'd be a great mother, but I don't think it's for everybody. And listen, I even feel the pressure of having only one kid! I was actually looking through the directory of Violet's school and trying to see how many only children there were. Not many. Most of the kids have "sibs," as they call them.

JANCEE: They call them "sibs"?

JULIE: That's the lingo. I also hate the term "only child." It just isn't a very nice way to put it. (*Sad, whispery voice*) I'm the *only one.* I'm all by myself.

JANCEE: (*whispery voice*) Won't someone play with me in my secret garden? I'm ever so alone. Whenever you hear that term, you picture some kid sitting on the floor, throwing a ball over and over against the wall, with no one to throw it back. Or quietly talking to a finger puppet and pretending it's a little brother.

JULIE: And there are only children who liked it and others who hated it. And then there's my dad, who had a sister when he was fifteen, so for all intents and purposes, he was an only child. And she died when he was fifty, so the idea of them being there forever for each other—well, that didn't happen. Did Tom like being an only child?

JANCEE: Yes. He liked reading alone in his room in peace—although this has continued through adulthood. He's very private, even with me sometimes.

JULIE: You should be glad about that.

JANCEE: Everybody else in my life shares everything, so it's okay by me.

JULIE: You don't need to hear every thought that ever went through his head. Although I like to hear every thought that goes through your head.

JANCEE: Oh, me too. Nothing is too trivial! I expect a full report later after you go to Costco with your Aunt Mattie, by the way.

JULIE: What's good is that I don't need anything this time. I can just get things for fun.

JANCEE: Like a sixty-ounce jar of pistachios. Let me tell you, you're such a relief to Tom. When I'm obsessing about something, he'll say, "Why don't you call Julie?" And he tries to say it in a light, friendly voice, but what he's really saying is, "Sweet Jesus, please let me finish the newspaper while you go examine every facet of your tiny problem with Julie for an hour and fifteen minutes on the phone." But to get back to kids, I know you love Violet and having her changed your life. And I know that it has actually brought you and Paul closer. Yet you've never, ever, given me the hard sell.

JULIE: I really think that a person who's happy with the decisions that they make, and is a good, conscious sort of person, should be able to let others do what they have to do without putting their own agendas on them. You know, one of the things that I tend to do when I'm feeling insecure about Violet being an only child is look around and think, *Other people with more kids seem to have a more normal life.* And then you come to find that no two people's experiences of the same thing are the least bit alike.

JANCEE: I do something similar when I find childless people. I always scan obituaries to see who didn't have kids, and then I try and figure out if they seemed to have had a happy and fulfilled life without them. Which is ultimately futile.

JULIE: It's hard to choose things that are so major in your life. I mean, I still get these nudgy feelings about having another child. Paul will say, "What if my mom had only had three kids? Then there would be no me." I mean, eventually you've got to stop! Someone's not going to be born.

JANCEE: I'm still trying to wrap my head around Paul's argument. I don't know how to even process that.

JULIE: I say to him, "You know what? Then the one your mother *didn't* have was the one who was scheduled to do the mass killing in Times Square." But I always thought my second kid was going to be a boy, who looked like me and had my personality. And it doesn't appear that I'm going to have that kid. And I do think, *Where's that soul?* And all of that kind of stuff.

JANCEE: I never knew that.

JULIE: I really do. Because I know that kid. But I can't do it. I keep asking the question and I can't. I don't think my body's up to it.

JANCEE: Well, then, maybe we're both done. (*Blows nose.*) Ugh, I have the worst cold. You still have yours, right? My nose is coming off in chunks. I keep putting Vaseline on it.

JULIE: I'll use my ChapStick and then quickly swipe it on my nose. If I'm not in public.

JANCEE: Yesterday I broke down and bought a neti pot—you know, the thing that you pour through your nasal cavity to irrigate it that yogis use? It felt like I was undergoing waterboard torture. I was struggling and choking.

JULIE: It's like you're drowning. But everyone I know loves them.

JANCEE: Not me. I whipped that thing into the trash in a rage.

JULIE: Well, I'm here at the gym.

JANCEE: Okay, then. Have a good workout. Talk to you after Costco.

8

Mister Soft E. Coli

When I first started dating a shy Chicago-born writer named Tom nine years ago, I knew within a month that I had to marry him. He went so far beyond my three core requirements (kind, funny, and intelligent) that I could hardly believe my good fortune. He was the rarest of men, the sort who truly had no idea he was classically handsome—six foot three, blue-eyed, cleft chin, fit from years of soccer, the works—and thus missing the arrogance I had grown wearily accustomed to in the New York City dating world. He was happiest with his nose buried in *New Scientist* magazine, or absorbed in researching an article on nineteenth-century iron-and-glass architecture.

I kept waiting for a hidden police report to surface, or evidence of a tiny conjoined twin that he had absorbed into his own body. But nothing untoward ever turned up. Kids and animals followed him around. He was a gourmet cook. Perhaps best of all, he was almost absurdly good-natured.

But as the years have rolled on, I've noticed that a change has come over my husband. I can deny no longer that the easygoing fellow I married has grown a bit more . . . what's the phrase? Ah, yes: *incredibly rigid.* His life is now governed by an ever-multiplying set of personal rules. They started cropping up in his late thirties. At the time, they seemed whimsically eccentric, like his refusal to enter a restaurant with the words *fun, factory,* or *eatery* in its name, or anything with a subtitle ("A Pan-Asian Fusion Bistro and Wine Bar").

But now that he has hit forty, I find I'm living in an iron cage of spousal predilection as he lists for me the things, as Winston Churchill once grammatically quipped, "up with which I will not put." So many, many rules: No whimsical boutique hotels ("Minibars are for bottles of Glenlivet, not condoms and Pez"). No Sunday brunches, which he terms "giving up the *New York Times* to wait in line for eggs in an enforced exercise in couplehood." Brands of jeans must have one name, or two at most (Levi's is acceptable, 7 for All Mankind is not). And he'll only see a film in the first five rows ("I can't lose myself in the story if I'm looking at rows of heads").

His inflexibility has even ruined the most carefree of summer traditions—buying an ice cream cone from a soft-serve truck on a hot day and idly eating it as you walk along. First of all, he will not eat ice cream in public; as he puts it, "walking while eating in general is weird." Ah. Second, he has product-cleanliness issues and calls our local Mister Softee truck "Mister Soft E. Coli." I used to put up a fight, but now I sigh in defeat and join him in eating ice cream from a reputable distributor, safely inside our apartment and away from the prying eyes of passersby.

Most of Tom's rules seem to center on order, quiet (if a television is blaring at our airport gate, he storms off to a TV-free gate nearby, so that we have to strain to listen for our flight announcement), and what he views as simple logic. I've heard similar complaints from dozens of women about their thirtyish and fortyish mates—men who, it should be noted, are otherwise reasonable, gentle, bookish types. It's just that certain situations seem to bring out a strain of stubbornness in them that borders on maniacal.

I know a woman who has lost friends because her husband will not attend any wedding with more than 150 guests (he has worked out some sort of complicated math involving seconds spent with the bride and groom versus his cost and time). My friend Jill has a husband who balks at clothing or accessories with logos (making gift shopping a particular challenge) and will not even consider seeing any movie that can be described as "life-affirming." Charlotte, another friend, must deal with a spouse who has decreed that no one in the family can speak loudly at breakfast. "Also, no newspapers can be delivered to the house, because it depresses him," she says. "If the temperature is between fifty and eighty degrees, the kids must play outside because when they play inside it depresses him. And I'm not allowed to tell him my dreams when I wake up."

Okay, I agree with him on that one. I have yet to hear a dream that's compelling. But is there not a thin line between being a little peculiar and being a tyrant? No younger man wants to be thought of as turning into his father, of being described by the dreaded term "set in his ways." Tom and I both chuckled, for instance, when we once took my parents on a driving tour of Scandinavia and my father brought along a Ziploc bag of Chex Mix the size of a throw pillow, as if Denmark was bereft of snacking opportunities, and a Thermos of his favorite Scotch, as if Sweden was a dry country. My father is the sort of man who ate Raisin Bran for breakfast for a full quarter-century until my mother persuaded him to made the radical switch to Kashi Good Friends (okay, Costco's bulk-purchase version). His loyalty to Consort for

Men hair spray has stretched back decades and will continue until he is spraying the one remaining hair on his head.

But wasn't my father's unwillingness to vary his routine just part of a continuum of hidebound male ritual that stretched to my husband's list of daily requirements, which is starting to resemble Kanye West's concert rider? What's the difference between a "young fogy," as he describes himself, and a standard-issue crotchety old fogy?

Tom maintains that because the men of his generation aren't the household autocrats of the fifties who demanded a silent martini after work, but rather the sort of evolved guys who use the word *parent* as a verb, his rules are annoying but ultimately harmless. His more romantic view is that they enclose him in a protective haven of civility, like Victorian-era British explorers who clung to their afternoon tea and biscuits, their phonographs and dusty book collections, even amid the most inhospitable foreign climes.

It's true that he actually does have tea at three o'clock every afternoon, no matter what country he happens to be in. And yes, I do understand why he won't use any product with the word *extreme* or *turbo* in it. But what, exactly, is "civilized" about "no movie sequels, ever, with the exception of *The Godfather* and *Star Wars*"? And can he really fight against patronizing stores with tip jars? He huffs that employers should pay their employees well instead of making them beg for tips, plus the sight of the jar "gives me general tip anxiety. Why stop at coffee shop employees? Why not tip the gas station attendant or the UPS man?"

Tom's rules have taken a toll on our relationship more than once. During a recent trip to Tokyo, the two of us got into a shouting match after dozens of restaurants failed to meet his criteria and we trudged for hours through the slate-colored rain. After he rejected one place for having fluorescent lights ("they make me nauseous and I can't enjoy my food") and another for its loud background music, I felt like I was trapped in an endless loop of *Rain Man*. I lost it. "I just want to eat dinner," I hollered miserably, as passersby gave us a wide berth. He wouldn't budge. Finally we found a ramen place that was to his liking.

Granted, those noodles, floating in rich, scallion-flecked broth, were . . . well, they were magnificent. But I wonder sometimes if I enable Tom's fussy behavior. I will admit to many quirks but no steadfast rules. None of my female friends have them, either, particularly if children are part of the picture. Kids' demands, they will tell you, have a way of preempting any oddball rules for living. "Women have to be more flexible and more forgiving," says my friend Tracy, whose boyfriend, a financial mogul, has a zero-tolerance policy toward flip-flops and phone calls "to check in."

It does seem hard to imagine a female version of Mr. Pink, Steve Buscemi's jittery character in *Reservoir Dogs*. In a famous scene set in a diner, he announces that he doesn't tip (again with the tipping, which comes up as much as brunch). "I don't believe in it," he barks. "I don't tip because society says I have to. If they really put forth an effort, I'll give them something extra, but this tipping automatically, it's for the birds. As far as I'm concerned she was just doing her job."

Maybe Mr. Pink clung to his no-tipping rule to avoid being engulfed by options paralysis. More than once, Tom has tried to explain his behavior by citing this famous phrase from Barry Schwartz's book *The Paradox of Choice*. Schwartz wrote of going to an electronics store and falling into a fugue state after being confronted with 110 different televisions and 85 different phones (and that was just for landlines). Tom likes to repeat Schwartz's argument that a tidal wave of choice leads to anxiety as we're haunted by second-guessing. To stave off that crippling ennui, why not keep it simple? When Tom goes into a Starbucks, he orders a large coffee with milk, period. No whipped cream. No espresso-truffle latte. No chocolate curls.

Of course, to a younger man, choice is enticing. But an older man is acquainted with disappointment. The years roll on, the regrets pile up, and suddenly your dogged adherence to "no alcoholic beverage that contains more than three ingredients" starts to make more sense.

"When I was younger, I was less discerning," says a male friend of mine. "But at this point in my life, I'm confident enough to trust my own taste." He adds that many of his seemingly random rules have actually improved his relationship with his wife. Oh? How is "only pre-1970-era jazz on long car trips" self-protective? "All arguments between couples on car trips begin with music preferences," he says. And what of "no talk of finances after five P.M.?" "I'll stay awake and brood, which interrupts her sleep. You see? I care about her getting enough rest."

Others claim that these rules protect their own health. My friend Lou can't abide laptops in coffee shops (home or library only), mirrors in restaurants, and being within ten yards of a Bluetooth earphone user (that last one in particular sends him into a molten rage). "For me, it's a way of decreasing stress in my life," he says. "If I compromise, I start a slow boil, and frankly, it's not good for me. At this point in my life, I'm well aware of my triggers, and unfortunately, I'm discovering new ones every day."

Tom, for his part, points to his semi-rootless existence. He's a writer who is always on the road, who lived in five New York apartments before we met, so he welcomes his self-imposed structure, even if it's theoretical. But surely it must go deeper than that. Could it have something to do with the nation's declining birthrate and the rise of only children such as Tom who simply like things their own way? Or Tom's long participation in Dungeons and Dragons as a youth (forgive me, Tom), which made him perhaps a little too adept at creating his own private, kooky world? In the end, there is probably a little truth in all of these theories.

And when Tom's rules wear me down, I console myself with his oft-repeated argument: At least with him, I know exactly what I'm getting.

I thought about a conversation I had with the Dungeon Master—er, Tom—in our Tokyo hotel after my street meltdown. When I accused him of taking a secret pleasure in winding me up, he looked at me with astonishment. "I'm not looking to torture you," he said. "Never. I just don't want to have bad experiences. And more important, I don't want you to have them either." It was as simple as that. After four decades on earth, time was no longer infinite for him. Those mediocre dinners and pointless films become less forgivable. And so, for Tom—and for me—out the window go reunion-concert tours, morning television, and invitations to events with vague dress codes like "smart casual" and "business festive."

In a grudging way, I suppose I admire this kind of moral absolutism, this willingness to stand one's ground despite raised eyebrows. It's better to be with a man who knows exactly what he likes than with some of the anything-goes guys of my past. The only thing more exhausting than being around someone with iron regulations is being around someone with none. It takes guts to stand by your principles, as uncool or outrageous as they may seem.

And for all of my husband's quirks, which sprout daily like Amazonian undergrowth in the rainy season, he's not so rigid in the ways that matter. He makes me laugh. He gamely accompanies me to the mall to buy place mats. On the aforementioned Scandinavian trip with my parents, he carted those people around in a tiny rental car for ten days as the air inside filled up with the sickly mint scent of their sugarless gum and the sound of my fa-ther's Julio Iglesias CD.

And maybe it's Tom's streamlining mechanisms that allow the intellectual part of his mind to flourish. He is the most curious person I know. He travels all over the world, reads four books a week. The important part of his mind is elastic, so I suppose I can deal with a quirk or two. Or fifty.

And so I accept without argument that there will be no view-ing of "Inspirational Coach" movies, ever. Unless it's on an air-plane. International flights only, six hours minimum.

9

Hug Them and
Squeeze Them for Me

My paternal grandma was the sort of well-groomed lady that I have always loved, the type who would never dream of leaving the house without every auburn hair firmly in place and a carefully blended circle of lipstick applied to both cheeks (if you lived through the Depression, rouge seemed an unnecessary extravagance). I used to see her once a year, because she lived across the country in Sun City, Arizona, a sprawling retirement community of forty thousand seniors who whiz around on golf carts, packing their Active Lifestyle with All That Jazz dance classes and cribbage games and pool aerobics.

So to keep in touch, I used to call her from my cubicle at *Rolling Stone* magazine, where I worked in the nineties. If I did an interview that went badly, it was particularly comforting to talk to her afterward. Fortunately she wasn't hard of hearing, so I was able to keep my voice down among my co-workers, who wouldn't necessarily think that calling Grandma was very "rock."

I once phoned her up after a dreadful encounter with the granite-faced members of Aerosmith. "Hi, Ma," I began. ("Ma," she felt, was a zippier moniker than "Grandma.")

"Well, hello, honey," she said in her gentle, creaky voice. "Are you at work?" She had answered on the first ring, as usual. My grandfather had died a few years prior, and while Ma liked to "keep busy," sometimes, she admitted, her afternoons were a little too still.

"Yes. I just tried for half an hour to get the guys in Aerosmith to talk at a red-carpet event. The more one-word answers I got, the more rambling my questions were. It was painful. The only nice one was the drummer."

"Well, that's often the case, isn't that what you told me?" I was always touched that Ma, whose musical tastes ran to the hymns she played on the church organ on Sundays, made an attempt to understand my world. It didn't matter that she had no idea who or what an Aerosmith was. I just liked it when she huffily declared that they were "ill-bred" and that it was not very professional of them to be rude to me.

I asked her how she was doing and slowly unclenched my teeth as she recited her recent activities: a morning at the beauty parlor to get her hair "fixed," a series of "nice lunches" with friends, a game of duplicate bridge. "You should smell the wonderful orange blossoms blooming here," she said. "They smell so good, although I have to go grab a handkerchief sometimes, as it seems I've developed an allergy." Later in the week, she and her sister, my great-aunt Lucile, were planning a banner day: a trip to their favorite thrift store ("we don't need a thing, but do you know, we can't *stop ourselves*"), a lunch buffet at their favorite gloppy-cheese-and-blobs-of-sour-cream Mexican place, and a spin through a model-home development, "just for fun." For Ma and her white-haired pals, model-home developments were amusement parks for seniors.

I had accompanied her on a few of these model-home larks in the past and always felt deep sympathy for the beleaguered sales reps forced to run through their spiel, room by room, for a horde of seniors who had not the slightest intention of buying. Instead they would remark in a loud voice, *Heavens, I surely don't know what I would do with all this space. Why on earth would you need a microwave that size? Honest to Pete, imagine the heating bill in here, Marianne, with these high ceilings. There goes your Social Security check.*

The exchanges I had with my grandma at that time had a civilizing effect on me, as if she had shown up in my grimy *Rolling Stone* cubicle and lightly placed a doily on my battered office chair.

I told my father about this rejuvenating effect one weekend at my parents' house, as we all sat around the kitchen shoveling handfuls of Costco snack mix into our mouths before dinner.

"I call her every Sunday, and I'm sure we hear the same details," he said. "Let me guess. She got her hair fixed and played duplicate bridge."

"Pretty much."

My father opened the pantry, wrestled out the four-pound container of snack mix, and unsteadily slopped more of it into the bowl. He told me that he used to phone his father at work. As both of them were proud employees of JC Penney at the time, naturally they liked to open with a round of shop talk. "We had these great conversations, and he became more of a friend than a father," he said. "You share different feelings you never could admit to when you were younger."

My grandfather died suddenly of a heart attack on his sixty-fifth birthday. A practical man, he had asked to be cremated immediately and interred in a wooden box to spare the family the cost of burial. The only problem with his plan was that the whole process happened so quickly that my dad never got to properly tell his father good-bye. He paused. "Do you know, I don't have anything recorded of his voice, ever? When I could have. It was possible. I'm sorry that I wasn't farsighted enough to record or even videotape him. I've got some old converted movies, but they don't have audio." He looked bleakly out the kitchen window. "It's one of those things that you put off until tomorrow, you're immersed in day-to-day living, and then all of a sudden tomorrow is there and you've missed the window. So that is a real regret of mine."

The three of us sat quietly for a bit. To break the silence, I asked my mother if she had any regrets about her own parents, Lillian and Hershal Corners, who had both died in the late seventies in the tiny Southern town of Citronelle, Alabama, where my mother was raised. To my surprise, she answered immediately that she had. While my father was the goopily sentimental type, fond of reminiscing and of poring for hours over old photos, my mother focused only on the present and the future. "I have no regrets about myself as a person," she said. "It's what I may have been able to do for my parents. I wish I could have done more for them financially, and I know that's irrational, because we didn't have any money. I regret that I didn't take my children down to Alabama more, because they worshipped you kids."

Even a few decades after their deaths, she could rarely talk about them without her voice catching. "You don't feel like an orphan when one dies, but you do for sure when both of them do," she said. "My emotional backup was gone. And also the person that rocked you, the only person that knew how you were as a baby, is gone. What kind of food did I eat? What dresses did I wear? They could be the only person in the world that knows that the reason why you're afraid of dogs is that you were attacked when you were six. And it's just . . . gone."

My mother was the youngest of six, the result of an accidental pregnancy, which my grandmother had originally assumed was some sort of tumor. She had my mother at the age of forty-two, an anomaly in those pre-IVF days, and as a result, my mother was the recipient of the sort of cosseting normally reserved for grand-children. This lavishing of affection only intensified when we girls came along. My grandparents had little money, but that didn't stop my grandma from slipping us twenties—cash it pains me to realize now that they could have really used. "Bless those girls' lit-tle hearts," she would say on the phone to my mother. "Hug them and squeeze them for me. You might even pinch them, sort of easy like."

When I was born, my parents lived in a tiny apartment in Rochester, New York, and my grandmother, wearing white gloves and a hat, took one of her few plane trips to "come and get hold" of me. "Mama had to stay in a hotel because we had only one bed-room, and when she got there, she was very upset that she left her gloves in the taxi," my mother recalled. "And wouldn't you know, the next morning the cabdriver knocked on our door and brought the gloves, telling me, 'I wanted that nice Southern lady to know that there are good Yankees, too.'" She dabbed away a little tear.

"So where is the regret? I don't understand."

She composed herself. "Well, we had saved up to serve her a steak. And she didn't tell me until years later that it took every-thing she had to eat that steak, because it was rare." She laughed. "So I regret that we didn't cook that steak to death."

I wiped a tear that dribbled down my own cheek. "Mom. Mom! You know that's irrational."

She nodded. "Of course." We reminisced for a while about her mother, whose only vices were smoking (she thought ladies didn't smoke, so only the immediate family witnessed her puffing away) and watching Saturday-night wrestling matches, especially the ones starring her absolute favorite, Gorgeous George. Then my mother sat upright.

"Come to think of it, you know what I might regret the most?" she said. "That I never asked her a question. Mama was eight when her mother died of pneumonia. She was one of ten children, and her father couldn't keep her in Virginia, where they lived at the time, so he sent her to live with his married sister in Alabama. And I have always wished that I asked her how she felt about that. Was she scared? How did she feel about losing her mother so young? I didn't want to make her feel bad because she would always tear up about it. But now I think that maybe I should have pressed her just a little." She picked at an imaginary piece of lint on her sleeve. "Because now I'll never know. She got married when she was sixteen. What was that like? I don't even know how she met my father. They had kids during the Depression, and so Dad had to move all over, pursuing jobs. I always wanted to know what she thought of that, too."

"Why didn't you ask?"

She shrugged. "I don't know. I don't know. Hers just wasn't a touchy-feely generation that shared all of that stuff."

That night, in my parents' guest room, I lay awake, preoccupied by what they had told me. It was difficult for me to grasp, in an age when no event is too small to be videotaped, the blunt finality of never hearing your father's voice again. It was harder still, as a member of the most analyzed generation in American history, to imagine shying away from questions that didn't seem remotely personal to me. The next day I continued to brood about it as I rode back to the city on an early New Jersey Transit train, so that I could go directly to the midtown offices of *Rolling Stone*.

As I slid into my chair, it occurred to me that because I often conducted one or more interviews a day, my tape recorder was permanently hooked up to my phone. Why couldn't I simply call my grandma in Sun City that afternoon and record our chat? And—at the risk of sounding creepily Nixonian here—I decided I would not tell her I was doing so. I have found that if you do, you will spend the first ten minutes listening to self-conscious fretting. *I don't know what to talk about. What should we talk about? What do you mean, "Just be yourself"? Are you recording this, right now? Seems kind of boring, doesn't it? Wait, can you go back and erase that last bit? I sounded stupid. Maybe you should turn it off until we really get going.* Even if the person eventually relaxes, the conversation never really loses that stiltedness.

I felt it was crucial that the exchange be natural, because when it comes to loss, what one often craves is not the significant events but the absolutely mundane. I can remember seeing an old Christmas videotape of our family grouped around the tree, waving and reciting *Merry Christmas, everybody!* Then my father turned the camera on each of us and asked about our plans for the coming year, which we dutifully answered. It was mildly interesting, but more for the clothes we were wearing than for the staged family assemblage and awkward answers. (Mom only granted us a glimpse of her real self at the end, when she told my father to turn the damn thing off, enough already.)

For me, the only compelling part of the entire tape occurred during the last five minutes. My father hadn't filled it up completely, so we kids grabbed the camera and filmed ourselves goofing off in the kitchen as we all made dinner. We had changed from our formal clothes into eighties leisure wear—Girbaud jeans and baggy, striped Esprit sweaters—and the kitchen counter was piled with the detritus of hectic family life. I studied that tape with the most intense longing, because there were the dishes we used at the time, and the puerile jokes we thought were fall-down funny, the hamburger-and-noodle casserole that we assumed was the pinnacle of haute cuisine. We were loose, and fully ourselves. It was the only genuinely authentic moment that existed on video from our youth.

And what is more intimate, more transporting, than a casual phone conversation between two people? And so I called Ma. Remembering what my father said, I talked to her for over an hour. Thinking of my mother, I asked Ma every question I could imagine. She told me about growing up on a farm in Council Grove, Kansas, and how she rode her horse, Ribbon, to school. I pulled out of her every detail about her wedding to my grandfather, which took place right in the parlor of her family home. She wore a modest brown dress and carried white flowers. When we got up to her experiences during World War II, we stopped.

Over the next year, I called her periodically and discreetly flicked on the tape recorder. I never did let her know. Her health began to decline soon after that, when she contracted pancreatic cancer. When she was in the last stages of this merciless, excruciating disease, my father flew out to Sun City and arranged for her to come home from the hospice where she had been staying. For the last week of her life, he fixed her the ice cream and lemon pudding that she loved, pulled up a chair next to the bed the hospice employees had set up in her home, and just talked with her quietly. He was holding her hand as she died.

A year or so later—about the time that your recollection of a loved one's voice begins to fade ever so slightly, despite your best intentions to fix it permanently in your mind—I handed my dad a little pile of tapes and a tape recorder. I wanted him to hear his mother's voice, before the morphine drip, before she had to be helped to the bathroom, but instead as she used to be, telling me one sunny afternoon that three hummingbirds had just flown onto her porch at the same time, do you believe it? Three! And they're so pretty. Why, they look like little jewels.

My dad smiled and hugged me. Then he poured himself a big glass of Scotch, put on a pair of headphones, went into his bedroom, and cried.

10

You Don't Have to Get Crazy

The phone rings at 9:07 A.M. It's Julie—who else?

JULIE: It's so windy out, you can't believe. I just saw a huge card-board box go flying down the street, smacking into things. It's a little Oz-like out here. So if you suddenly hear nothing, it's me taking off entirely. So how are you?

JANCEE: I'm not in a good mood today, for some reason.

JULIE: Well, I know why I'm not. My mom was just visiting for three nights. It's always chaotic. There were whirlwinds of stuff everywhere, and for every minute, she has a new glass on the table. And she wears this lipstick that doesn't come off, ever—like, she wakes up in the morning and has lipstick on. But it does come off on my glasses. So I have to scrub the glass before I put it in the dishwasher so I don't see my mother's lip print every time I have a drink.

I'm going to start right off the bat here with my morning pet peeve, which is people who say "What part of *no* don't you understand?"

JANCEE: I'm with you on that one. I'm with you.

JULIE: Especially when they tell you about how they said it to somebody else. I was just listening to my super talking, and he's one of those people who always has a big mouth—in the stories in his mind, that is.

JANCEE: "So I look him right in the eye and say to him—"

JULIE: "What part of *no* don't you understand?"

JANCEE: I notice we both talk about our supers a lot.

JULIE: That's because we both have Schneiders in our buildings.

JANCEE: It's true. So yesterday, when I'm working, my parents call on their car speakerphone. Because now, whenever they don't have a book on tape handy, I become the book on tape. There was an early snowstorm, so they called from McDonald's, where they pulled over to wait for the trucks to salt the roads. And I felt pressure to keep them occupied. (*Sighs.*) They used to call me individually, but now they're always on speakerphone, where I can't hear their responses because it's a bad connection and my voice echoes. And it's my mother doing ninety-five percent of the talking and my father mostly complaining about the traffic. Do your parents do this?

JULIE: They only do speakerphone if it's "news." Instead, my parents both have a phone on either side of their bed. One of them has a cordless and the other has a regular phone—you know, just in case of emergencies? And sometimes when they both talk, there are weird delays, so it sounds like my dad is in Belize and my mother is in Uzbekistan, combined with him telling her that she's talking too loud and vice versa, and her telling him to get off the phone and go brush his teeth.

JANCEE: If my father answers the phone at home, he'll say, "Wait, your mother is getting on the other line." And the strange thing is, while we wait, he doesn't make chitchat. We just sit in silence.

JULIE: He doesn't do hold music for you, like we do for each other? (*Hums elevator music.*) Sometimes when I tell one parent a story, the other will say, "Start from the beginning, from when you walked in, and . . ." And both of them already know the story because one has already *told* the other! But they want to hear it in my words. My mother will make me sometimes tell a story forty times if it involves a compliment to either her or me. "Tell me again what they said." (*She pauses while a siren blares.*) I have to take a little minute here to tell you that I'm at a Hundredth and Broadway, and the other night a car drove into the Indian restaurant here on the corner. So it's all boarded up, but they have a huge sign that says WE'RE OPEN. Beckoning you to come in to the side that isn't boarded up, for a little chicken tikka with glass.

JANCEE: They shouldn't have boarded it up. Then you could have just stepped through the hole. It's more welcoming.

JULIE: Anyway. When my parents do call me on speakerphone, my father thinks that anytime the phone rings, it's time for him to start a meal.

JANCEE: My parents do that, too. It's like dinner theater.

JULIE: And even if my father is talking to the president of the United States, he's still going to chew loudly. I think he keeps a little jar of corn nuts right by the phone. He makes this mixture of corn nuts and wasabi peas. That's his Chex Mix. (*Imitates him crunching loudly.*)

JANCEE: My sister Heather called my mother the other day to ask her a question: If she was only a B cup, was it necessary to throw on a bra to run to the grocery store? And my mother said no, and then Heather hears my father say, "You know, I think it's fine not to." And she said, "Dad, were you actually listening to this conversation?" Then she heard a click as he quickly hung up.

JULIE: "Oh, that wasn't your dad!"

JANCEE: Is it too much to ask to identify yourself?

JULIE: There are just areas you don't want your dad involved in. That would never happen to me because there's no way that you can miss the crunching, the slurping, the brushing of teeth. But here's my other pet peeve. You're talking to them and they're talking to each other at the same time under their breath. (*Imitates them with muttering voice.*) "Have you seen it?" "No, I already put it in there." (*To Julie*) "No, I was listening, go on." (*Muttering voice*) "You start walking, I'll meet you." The multitasking, the conversations. You're not entertaining *me,* people.

JANCEE: That's what happened to me yesterday when my parents were bickering about whether they had a McDonald's coupon in the car or not! (*Imitates Southern mother in trademark Foghorn Leghorn voice.*) "Jay, it's in the coupon book, and I'm telling you, we left it at home. Yes, it is. Yes, it most *suh-tainly is.* It's in the junk drawer." They got so swept up in their power struggle that they completely forgot I was there.

JULIE: My mother hates when you call and she's watching a movie on TV at night, but she can't stand to possibly hurt your feelings by saying "I'm watching a movie." And she doesn't pause it, either. My favorite one of all time was when I called her—this is going back a few years—and she was watching *Seinfeld.* I said, "I can tell you're watching *Seinfeld,* so why don't you watch it and we'll talk another time." And she says, "Okay. Me too."

JANCEE: Are you serious?

JULIE: I hung up and then called back a minute later so I could tell her what had just happened. Because, you know, you need a fresh call to get their attention again. With the other call, I had already lost her. I had to be a new person.

JANCEE: So they never call you from the car?

JULIE: My mother does and she uses a Bluetooth.

JANCEE: I'm impressed.

JULIE: Don't be, because the phone conversation is almost always about making the phone work. "I don't know if I need a new charger. I feel like I charge this thing all the time and it says, 'Low battery'! Can you hear me?"

Did I tell you? Last night we're at my house, and I'm sitting at the table with Violet doing something, and the phone keeps ringing, so I keep running over to answer it, and my mother finally says, "No, no, it's just me trying my cell phone, don't answer it." And I'm like, *Why are you calling my house? Can't you check it with somebody who will pick it up?* Then I check my phone later and I have forty-two messages of her checking her cell phone.

JANCEE: My mom has a code where she calls three times and hangs up. So I run to answer it and miss it. Then I go back to the living room and do something else and it happens again, and I miss it.

JULIE: What's the purpose of the code?

JANCEE: Their phone comes up as "private caller," so I think she thinks this sends a special signal.

JULIE: Then you'll know it's her and race to answer it. My father, even though he and everybody else in the world has voice mail, still leaves these messages: "It's Dad, hello. Hello! Anybody there? Hello, it's Dad." I'm like, *There's nobody to hear you.* And my parents have voice mail themselves! Somehow he's envisioning 1986 with the separate machine in the room and us screening.

JANCEE: For years my father did the same thing. "Pick up! I'll wait here a minute."

JULIE: You know what I also noticed about my mother? Whenever I call her and tell her something that I'm going to do—for instance, when I told her I'm going to make chocolate chip cookies, so I'm buying some new cookie sheets because mine are burnt—my mother says, "You don't have to get crazy." It means doing anything that veers off the path of walking one straight line. If I say, "I really want to read that article in the paper," she'll say, "You don't have to get crazy with it."

JANCEE: What's the proper response to that?

JULIE: You just have to say, "I'll try my best not to get crazy." I don't know. A lot of what she says I just ignore. What else is going on today?

JANCEE: I'm trying today to hold off on eating an early lunch. Yesterday I ate lunch at 11:20 A.M. When Tom's away and I set my own schedule, I move everything forward a few hours. Do you know what time I had dinner last night? Five-fifteen. I wish I was kidding, but I'm not. I just can't wait to eat.

JULIE: There's not a thing wrong with that. Not a thing!

JANCEE: And do you know what else I'm doing? Ordering new towels.

JULIE: Don't tell me.

JANCEE: Yes! One day, my towels just started smelling weird. Just like yours did last month. What is that about?

JULIE: It's a mystery. It's not like your washer/dryer changes.

JANCEE: And it's not like I've done anything different, like host a football team or anything. And once those towels start reeking, it's over. You just have to buy new towels.

JULIE: All right, I'm at the gym. I'll call you when I get out. Remind me to go to the health-food store because sometimes when I'm talking to you on the way home, I forget to do my stops.

JANCEE: I'll remember. Have a good workout.

11

Secure Your Wig with Extra Hairpins Before Lovemaking

My mother, as I have mentioned elsewhere, is a former beauty queen. She was one of Mobile, Alabama's Azalea Trail Maids, an honor reserved for the prettiest and most accomplished local girls, who are selected to dress in candy-colored antebellum costumes and act as "official ambassadors" to the city. More notably, she was crowned the 1960 Oil Queen of Citronelle, Alabama. Her dedication to proper deportment and good grooming continues to this day. Not once have I seen her slop around the house past 8 A.M. in a bathrobe and slippers, whereas my at-home uniform is best described as Mommy Drinks.

Like many children of glamorous mothers, I used to love to watch her apply makeup in front of the bathroom mirror before a big night out. The problem was that she was so skillfully efficient—in a way that only a beauty queen can be—that the whole ritual was over in a matter of minutes. I needed more. And, as a Garanimals-clad kid with freckles and an overbite that would soon require braces, I frankly needed help.

Then I discovered a book called *Polly's Principles.* It sat dustily on the shelf of my tiny local library, which didn't have the cash to update its Beauty, Health, and Diet section with more current tomes. The subtitle was *Polly Bergen Tells You How You Can Feel and Look as Young as She Does.* I was twelve years old and had no idea as to the identity of Ms. Bergen, but her photo on the cover seemed attractive enough. Nor did I, as a prepubescent, have a pressing need to look young. But to my mind, anyone older and more experienced than I was an authority, so I took the book home and scrupulously followed Bergen's brisk instructions. At the time, I didn't realize that many of her principles were exuberantly, spectacularly nuts.

Ms. Bergen began the book on a warmly empathetic note. "I hear some of you saying right now, 'OK, but what can a woman like Polly Bergen tell *me,* with *my* problems?'" she wrote. "'What do I have in common with a show-business personality and successful business executive who gets around in places that I only read about and meets people who are only names to me in the newspapers and magazines?'"

Polly then relayed her inevitable tale of triumph, of a bullied small-town girl who eventually landed glamorous film roles and a coveted long-standing gig as a panelist on *To Tell the Truth.* It was a long, rough road, God knows it was, but along the way, she learned how to put herself together.

I paged through the book in happy abandon, lost in Ms. Bergen's Hollywood tales and exotic advice. One maxim: Inspect your naked body *every single day* for defects. Polly gave her "derriere" a rigorous daily once-over for "crepeyness [*sic*]," then moved on to her legs to detect any emergent varicose veins, and finally to her stomach to catch any folds. Another valuable lesson: Always use two colors of lipstick, such as "orange mat [*sic*]" and "orange frost." It seemed that Polly could face down any beauty crisis. Have an unsightly wart on your face? Use an eyebrow pencil to turn it into a large, brown, three-dimensional beauty mark!

Her chapter on sensuality was particularly intriguing to my young mind. She urged readers to paint their nipples with lipstick, and to skip the "crotch deodorant" in favor of your distinctive female aroma, which would drive your man wild. I had only a vague idea of what a crotch deodorant was, but I made a careful note to avoid it. The free-spirited actress was also against wearing underwear. Instead, she bought pants with shields sewn into the crotch (clearly she had an affinity for the word *crotch*) or, if said shields were not present, she picked up a couple at the "notions counter."

Moving on to skin care, Ms. Bergen warned readers to shun cigarettes, even as she puffed away herself and cheerfully confessed no real desire to quit, even when Cary Grant harassed her to do so. Most of her skin advice, however, appeared to be a plug for the Polly Bergen Company, a skin-care and cosmetics concern whose trademark ingredient in those pre-conservationist times was turtle oil (or, as the company alluringly put it, Oil of the Turtle).

The final chapter ended on a rueful, bittersweet note with the title "I'm Going to Love Myself Someday." I closed *Polly's Principles* with a satisfied sigh. This book had it all: entertaining Hollywood tidbits (Jerry Lewis once horrified Polly by calling her an old hooker), inspiring perseverance (maybe I, too, could improve my average looks enough to decamp to Hollywood!), relatable neuroses (Polly hated her short legs, straight ankles, and low-hanging behind). And, of course, there were plenty of useful beauty tips, such as Polly's exhortation to avoid the sun (even as she admitted to crispily frying her own skin for years).

Well. Celebrity beauty-and-exercise books had hooked me for life.

In the eighties, a slew of them had been released by model-slash-actresses, and I petitioned my library to order them all: Victoria Principal's *The Beauty Principal,* Jaclyn Smith's *The American Look,* Cheryl Tiegs's *The Way to Natural Beauty.* Each followed the same trajectory: sad tales of teenage unattractiveness (even as Principal supplied a photo of herself looking poised and lovely at age sixteen, a year before her good looks landed her in commercials), chatty, confidential stories of criticisms from callous casting agents and modeling scouts, followed by hard-won wisdom. The books usually closed with some sort of wry epilogue on how the star had come to love herself, dammit, although some days—hell, most days—it was not easy. It was not easy.

I followed their advice with the utmost dedication. Who, if not Cheryl Tiegs and Jaclyn Smith, possessed the magical secrets of Looking Your Very Best? At nighttime in my bedroom, I'd dutifully go through their recommended calisthenics, getting down on my hands and knees and counting out twenty-five donkey kicks for each leg. I slathered a refrigerator's worth of homemade masks—eggs and oatmeal and lemons—onto my face, sure that my zits would disappear to reveal glowing skin like Victoria's. I ate dreary breakfasts of dry wheat toast, a half grapefruit, and unsweetened coffee, hoping that the large-curd cottage cheese on my legs would be replaced with Tiegs-quality thighs.

At first I made careful notes from each library book and put them all in a Trapper Keeper, but eventually I began a home collection, for handier referral. The first book was given to me by my parents: Brooke Shields's *On Your Own,* a treatise on looking good during one's college years, written after Brooke's first year at Princeton in the mid-eighties. My mother knew that I used to pore over any *Seventeen* magazine that featured the *Blue Lagoon* star on the cover.

The book was an unpleasant shock. How could this sultry model whose pouty Calvin Klein jeans ad graced my bedroom wall be so eye-wateringly boring? It's no stretch to imagine that her wooden wholesomeness was a response to her background as a child film star who played a prostitute at thirteen, a kid whose notorious mother/manager once compared her nubile daughter to a work of art that everyone should be able to contemplate. Yet somehow her book grew on me, maybe because her advice was so endearingly square, with many earnest lectures on resisting peer pressure and remaining true to oneself. While others may have spent the Reagan era waking up to a morning bong hit with the stranger they had picked up the night before, studious Brooke, whose circle of friends included Bob Hope and Wayne Newton, was busy being the least hip college sophomore in the United States of America.

It's hard not to wonder what Brooke's dorm-mates thought of her, particularly when she divulged her method of coping with stress: listening to a tape that a fan sent her of "wonderful old accordion music." She didn't drink, smoke, stay out late, or touch sugar or dairy; one famous section in the book is titled "What My Virginity Means to Me." In it, Brooke candidly admitted that she was scared to get intimate with a man (presumably her terror and confusion only increased after she dated both Michael Jackson and George Michael) and urged uncertain readers to take their time, too. Even if she hadn't spelled out her uncharted sexual status, one glance at the photo she supplied of her college bedroom, with its frilly flowered lampshades and Cabbage Patch doll, told you everything you needed to know.

But Brooke was not all self-denial. Sometimes, she wrote, her fun-loving Princeton classmates threw chartreuse parties, in which everyone had to . . . well, wear chartreuse, you see. (Brooke joined in the madness by putting on some chartreuse eye shadow and chartreuse fishnets.) But mostly she was incredibly disciplined, striving not to go a single day without exercise and avoiding the freshman fifteen by visualizing her mother appearing in the dining hall, watching her daughter's every bite as she sat next to a giant scale. She counseled late-night studiers to fill up on carrots and celery rather than cookies. The whole book was like a demure letter of advice from Grandma, yet all of the photos were taken by such legendary fashion photographers as Patrick Demarchelier and Albert Watson.

Which brings me to another reason why I cherish these books: Even the most primly sensible tome can't suppress the ego and sheer kookiness present in even the most levelheaded famous person. Enterprising readers can always find beautifully telling details of these stars' personal lives buried in the diet and hair tips. (Do *you* keep weight off by imagining your disapproving mother next to a giant scale? What, exactly, was going on in that relationship?)

Sometimes these nutty biographical details aren't buried at all. In Joan Crawford's *My Way of Life* (in my view, the undisputed classic of the genre), she is blazingly frank about her control issues. Joan, of course, was a steely perfectionist who determinedly transformed herself from skinny Lucille LeSueur, product of a broken San Antonio home, into a sleek Hollywood star, and her continuing, obsessive quest for Total Excellence practically radiated off the pages. Known for showing up to every film set early and for scrubbing down the toilets of every hotel she stayed in, Joan ran her life with military precision and dictated that you do the same.

One of her many revealing anecdotes was her livid reaction when three guests dared to show up at her New York penthouse apartment without an invitation (something, she noted, that her own children would *never think* of doing). This was *not* in the schedule her secretary was told to plan out three months in advance! She had just enough time to run to her dressing room, furiously whip on some lipstick, and don a "lovely dress that I had bought in Canada" before receiving her thoughtless, impulsive visitors.

Apparently, Joan's Way of Life was to wring usefulness and productivity out of every waking moment. Read your newspaper standing up as you do isometric exercises! Walk around the house with toes pointed inward for crucial extra leg toning! Sitting at a desk? Roll a bottle back and forth under the arches of your feet to slim the ankles! Do impromptu ballet moves while vacuuming! Better yet, simultaneously wear a nourishing mayonnaise mask on your face!

Mayonnaise was one of her many beauty-enhancing kitchen-made remedies. "For years I washed my daughters' hair with raw eggs, never soap or shampoo," she wrote. "I wet their hair first and then rubbed in six whole eggs—a trick I learned from Katharine Hepburn." I understood the practicality of her tip of using a thick layer of petroleum jelly as a makeup remover—gooey but a money saver—but were half a dozen eggs per child more economical, or easier, than shampoo? Well, Joan must have had her reasons.

As for diet, the ultra-disciplined star avoided sugar, so much so that in a scene from *What Ever Happened to Baby Jane?* in which her character was supposed to be munching chocolates, she recalled that she made some tiny meatballs at home and brought them in to eat on camera instead. Wasn't protein better than empty calories, after all?

If Joan's book displayed the most lunacy, Elizabeth Taylor's engaging diet tome, *Elizabeth Takes Off,* had the most personality. She struck the perfect balance between glamour (she dedicated the book to, among others, terminally suave actor Robert Wagner and *Dynasty* gown designer Nolan Miller) and the sort of genuine candor most celebrities would never dare attempt. No wonder the book sold petrillions upon its 1987 release (my mother kept a pristine copy for years and used many of Liz's recipes, including the poached garlic chicken and the artificial-sweetener-powered "chocolate fantasy"). There's so much to love in this book: Liz's colorful, chaotic biography, which kicks off the proceedings, is so extensive, so replete with *passions* (Richard Burton! Diamonds! Rubies! Fried chicken and mashed potatoes!), that she doesn't even get down to the business of dieting until page 111.

This is a woman who dug into life with refreshing gusto. One of my favorite photos of Ms. Taylor is a snap of her and Richard Burton messily eating burgers together, descending upon them with the same zeal with which they fell upon each other. One is reaching for the ketchup. It's the sexiest, most romantic picture I've ever seen. But what makes this book so relatable is that Elizabeth, as we all must, paid heavily for her earthy appetites. The volume's saddest portion detailed life with her sixth husband, Virginia senator John Warner. When they married in 1976, Liz found herself thrown into the disorienting world of politics as she joined him on the grueling, fried-food-strewn campaign trail. She had already gained weight from bad hotel room service when he was elected to the Senate in 1976, and thereafter kept piling it on as she turned to food to alleviate boredom. The most wretched line in the whole book, as far as I'm concerned, occurred during her description of the deathly quiet nights at home with Warner in D.C., a bleak contrast with the whirling social scene in Los Angeles.

"Most evenings," she wrote, "he'd say, 'Why don't you go upstairs and watch TV, Pooters'—his nickname for me—'I've got so much to do I just don't know when I'll finish."

There is so much pathos in that little scene. *Pooters.* Not a very sexy nickname, was it? Would you want to be called Pooters? And he's basically telling her, not unkindly, to run along now. It was a grim picture, this celebrated Hollywood star, trudging upstairs in her caftan for another night of Carson.

And so she eventually ballooned to 180-plus pounds. She wasn't shy about presenting photographic evidence in the book, either, accompanied by tart captions, or of describing her face as "suet" and likening her body to a great white whale. (But of course, just when things got too pedestrian, George Hamilton or Rock Hudson dropped by, or an enormous Bel Air mansion was purchased.)

Elizabeth's moment of reckoning arrived after a hard look in a full-length mirror. Eventually she whittled herself down to 122 pounds through diet ("a bore") and a grudging exercise program tailored to her bad back. She rewarded herself with a weekly, pornographically described "pig-out," which might consist of an entire pizza followed by a hot fudge sundae, which she rightly pointed out is only properly festive if there is more hot fudge than ice cream. And, like a true celebrity, Elizabeth borrowed "one day at a time" principles from AA to apply to dieting. (Her alcoholism, she claimed, would be a different book entirely, one that I will certainly snap up.)

Joan Collins was another tempestuous, oft-married brunette, whose 1980 beauty-and-fitness book became a cornerstone of my collection. *The Joan Collins Beauty Book,* the first of five lifestyle guides that the industrious *Dynasty* star churned out, is my most prized because it's such a decadent, spandex-body-suited-and-terrycloth-headbanded time capsule. While today's beauty and fitness guides are penned by a tedious parade of chipper personal trainers and nutritionists who favor chapter titles like "The Joy of Soy," Joan's book was more suited for undoing the damage of staying out all night at Regine's. "I pay attention to the upkeep of my health and looks, but not to the detriment of my enjoyment of life," she wrote, "and this includes eating well, drinking wine, staying up late, sunbathing, and even, God forbid, smoking!"

Show me another beauty guide that includes a "tip" to stay away from cocaine, which could sap a girl's looks. (Joan related her own story of doing blow in Saint-Tropez, after which she was plagued by insomnia and a nasty case of postnasal drip.) And who but the woman who played Alexis Carrington would devote an entire page to wig maintenance, a section criminally absent from most beauty books? (Be sure and secure your wig with extra hairpins, she cautioned, before "lovemaking.") Even the section on vitamins had a debauched, Studio 54 feel: Joan confided that if she had been smoking heavily, she took up to nine thousand milligrams of vitamin C as a restorative. The disco ball continued to whir in the skin-care section, when she shared an effective tanning formula from her youth: Mix eight parts baby oil with one part iodine; apply every hour. This, she warned responsibly, should not be done too often, but she admitted that it did provide a "gorgeous glowing tan."

Heavy perfume received a well-deserved nod, too. Ms. Collins, a fan of major Statement Scents like Opium and Jungle Gardenia by Tuvache, urged readers to layer it on with abandon: Start with perfumed soap and bath oil in the tub, followed by a dousing of scented powder, body lotion, and cologne, and *then* a liberal dose of the perfume itself. Why be timid? Announce yourself in a hurricane of overpowering scent, the olfactory equivalent of enormous shoulder pads! If people flee from you in the elevator with handkerchiefs over their mouths, why, then, you have it all to yourself!

Joan knew how to maintain her allure. She wore fishnet stockings and a full face of evening makeup for her exercise photos and unapologetically listed her most trusted crash diets: the six-eggs-a-day diet, the banana-and-milk diet (Joan lost a quick seven pounds on this one when she first signed with Twentieth Century–Fox), and the nothing-but-green-grapes plan. Unsure if a crash diet is for you? Joan provided a simple test: Lie flat on your back and put a ruler lengthwise on your stomach. If it doesn't form a straight ridge between your pubic bone and your ribs, better stock up on those grapes.

In the mid-eighties, celebrity beauty books became a little more workmanlike. While ones written in the sixties encouraged artifice and drastic diet shortcuts, the eighties ushered in an era of frisky outdoorsiness. This is best exemplified by *Christie Brinkley's Outdoor Beauty and Fitness Book,* which I loved when I was younger and now find completely exhausting. Christie, while a joy to behold in a bathing suit, wouldn't necessarily be the most fun companion on a vacation. "How often have you sat in the sand watching the surf crash or listening to the radio?" she wrote. "You could have been exercising!" Every paragraph burbles with energy and bristles with exclamation points. There are endless photos of her working out on various sunny beaches, battling what she calls "El Bulgo" and smiling wide enough to display her back molars.

The supermodel used every opportunity to enhance her splendor. After a beach party, she liked to procure half a can of flat beer from the bar and comb it through her hair as a makeshift setting lotion, and was fond of using cut lemons to rub on her elbows. (After ten minutes, they'll be "bleached white!")

Christie's book, along with fellow eighties model Cheryl Tiegs's *The Way to Natural Beauty,* could be useful, although neither was as appealingly quirky as their predecessors. When I revisited Tiegs's guide not long ago, the only read-entertainingly-aloud nuggets were descriptions of her early binge eating. She related the story of being on a bathing-suit shoot in Puerto Rico and finding some ancient boxes of crackers in the cupboard of a house she was renting. Insects were literally hatching inside the crackers, so resourceful—and hungry—Cheryl simply ate around the bugs. Fabulous!

Another spree involved a box of cookies that one of her New York City roommates had received from Paris. The roommate had eaten the "gooey insides" of the cookies and tossed the chewed-up crusts into the garbage bin. "When I got home that night," Cheryl recalled, "I caught a glimpse of those castaways and one by one extracted them from the garbage and finished them off. Some had the flavor of orange peels, others of coffee grind." Why was it so gruesomely comforting to read about her moments of weakness?

I had the opposite feeling when I recently tracked down Jaclyn Smith's *The American Look*. I remember taking scrupulous notes from my library copy and carefully following her instructions to wash my hair with a final blast of freezing water to maintain its shine. But when I reread the book, I discovered a chilliness my youthful eyes had missed. One paragraph breezily began with "Despite my good fortune in having little trouble maintaining my ideal 115 pounds . . ." She went on to say that she was blessed with "untroubled skin," she was "not troubled" by eye redness; exercise was a pleasure; and her pregnancy didn't show until she was six months along. These declarations were bolstered with photos of Jaclyn looking regal as she lounged by the pool, toes fetchingly pointed. Jaclyn had broken the crucial covenant with readers of these sorts of books. What she was required to do was pretend she wasn't an otherworldly creature blessed by genetics in order to sell the illusion that looks like hers were actually achievable with contouring makeup and half a grapefruit for breakfast. If Jaclyn had only confessed to wolfing down half-gnawed cookies studded with old coffee grinds, her book might still be in print.

My collection stopped as the nineties commenced and these books fell out of fashion. Now the star is either the diet itself—South Beach, the Mediterranean Diet—or an all-business personal trainer. How could they compare to *Super Looks,* Morgan Fairchild's classic 1984 guide in which she vamps on the cover in glittering jewels, a sequined bustier, and two crimson slashes of blush on her cheekbones? Give me three dozen lavish photos of a celebrity doing halfhearted, low-impact, sweat-free aerobics in a fuchsia leotard, matching leg warmers, and a full face of inappropriate evening makeup. (If she's holding a matching fuchsia set of half-pound weights, so much the better.)

And so I cling to my old collection and revel in its datedness. Reading these musty old books brings me a perverse pleasure as I marvel at how seriously I followed the frequently bonkers advice. I was so hopeful that I could actually get rid of my freckles with a few squirts of lemon juice and vanquish my paunch with eight glasses of water a day.

And I realized recently that my mother has had a much greater influence on my appearance than any model or movie star. It was she who instilled in me my most enduring habits, from dressing well on a budget to a healthy dollop of sunblock even on cloudy days. Her longest-running campaign, met with mild but not overwhelming success, has been a protracted attempt to convert her daughters from the natural look to the more vivid makeup that she favors. When it comes to cosmetics, my mother has always believed that it's pretty much impossible to overdo it. In fact, if she had written her own book—let's call it *Judy's Principles*—it would include the following:

- Sit up straight. Slouching makes you look like you have saggy bosoms.

- Get that gum out of your mouth. Hold on a minute, I've got a tissue in my purse. We are *not* going into this restaurant with you chewin' your cud like a cow. It makes a person look less intelligent. It just does. Put your gum in this tissue. I'm not arguing with you.

- If you have a chocolate craving, just eat the tiniest, tiniest little handful of chocolate chips. I always keep a bag right in the pantry for emergencies.

- Stop fiddling with your hair. (*Sound of hand briskly slapping away daughter's hand*) You look like a teenager when you do that.

- I don't know what you girls have against brooches. It's the best way to add personality to an outfit.

- Don't overpluck those eyebrows of yours, or they will never grow back. You'll have spindly little eyebrows forever. Is that what you want?

- Your generation takes this whole "natural look" too far. A little eye shadow never hurt anyone. I do *not* say that all the time. What's so funny? Honest to Pete, you girls laugh at everything I say. Let me show you. Come here and hold still. This is called "Midnight" by Clinique. Now. Doesn't that look better?

12

Don't Be Weird

I ask you: If my definition of total happiness is a long trip to Japan, or India, or Morocco, then why is it that I can't manage to leave my apartment when I'm in America? I never want to go anywhere. I can barely cope with a trip to the dry cleaner. I just want to stay home. Scarily, I can do so for days and days and days. What is this cabin fever I hear about? I once interviewed country star Martina McBride, who admitted that she, too, often had to be flushed out of her lair. I asked her how long she has hunkered down at home without leaving. When she told me a week, I nodded soberly and squeezed her arm in understanding. If I had a platinum-record-built Nashville compound like Martina's, I could easily dig in for a month.

Not that I have a bad setup at the moment. I live in a converted church, a venerable old structure nearly a block long. It was built as South Congregational Church in the 1850s—Henry

Ward Beecher was said to have preached there—but by the 1980s, its flock had sadly dwindled and the church was sold to a developer. Now there are thirty condos inside, but from the outside it still looks like a house of worship and frequently confuses deliverymen. The building is wonderfully quiet because of its massive stone walls, and its earlier incarnation gives the place a tranquil feel. And so I tend to stay put.

Julie shares the same strain of agoraphobia. "Why leave?" she'll say sensibly. "For what?" Home is a guaranteed good time. You can read. You can watch a movie. You can make brownies. You can take a nice bubble bath. As Pascal said, "Man's unhappiness springs from one thing alone, his incapacity to stay quietly in one room." Why leave? For what?

Forget parties, which I view as work. The irony is that even as a card-carrying hermit, I am still pleased to be invited places, and appreciative of anyone who makes the effort to host any sort of shindig, a nightmare I would never bring on myself. I know already I'd be the type of host who would obsess about the one guest who isn't screaming with laughter, making out with strangers, and spraying everyone with jets of champagne. So I show up to any place I'm invited and then make everyone uncomfortable as, filmed with sweat, I strain to be the witty and sparkling bon vivant, the spirited initiator of a thousand lively conversations. I solicit opinions. I ask questions.

Sometimes this approach works too well. I once sat next to a man at a dinner party and threw out some of my regular starters: Where did you last go on vacation? Do you have any horrible neighbors? (All New Yorkers like to talk about their horrible neighbors.) He answered eagerly enough but never asked anything in return. To amuse myself, I started counting up my inquiries. When I reached question number thirty (at which point I wanted to holler *Pop quiz! What's my name? Where am I from? I don't need a state, just give me a general region!*) I turned with a sigh to the person on my other side.

I usually spend the cab ride home from any gathering recovering from social anxiety disorder. "What the hell is with people?" I carped recently to Tom after a cocktail party where I spent ten minutes in a group that talked around and above me. When I was finally able to break in and introduce myself, I was quickly assessed and dismissed. Then they all resumed speaking as if I weren't there. "Why can't people engage in a simple conversation? Is this a New York City problem? Is it an East Coast thing? Is it modern society?"

Tom didn't answer and wearily closed his eyes. "You know what's worse?" I went on. "Either people ice you because they can't figure out a way you can be useful to them, or they overshare. How about the woman who told us she just had unprotected make-up sex with her heroin-addicted ex-boyfriend? We met her five minutes before she yielded that one up! Yet I found myself asking her follow-up questions to be polite. I asked her if they went on any more dates after that. Then she laughed at me because I called them 'dates'! What was I supposed to call them? Encounters? Appointments?" I slumped in my seat. "God, I hate myself."

Tom gazed out the window. He had heard this jabber many times. "You really don't have to try so hard," he said. Tom, unlike many of my friends, never wastes time on postgame analysis. The most I have typically been able to coax out of him is confirmation that an event was fun, or not fun. Then the subject is closed, whereas I tend to fret about my shoddy performance for at least an hour.

I looked broodingly out my window of the taxi. "I shouldn't have asked that blond woman so many questions about her dead dog. But she seemed to want to talk about it. Was it me? She worked that dead Chihuahua into every conversation. I just felt like she needed an ear. But then did you see how upset she got? She broke away and ran to the bathroom."

Tom shook his head. "I don't know what gets into you." Tom is very different from my friends and family. If I relay my latest gaffe to one of them, they will helpfully construct an elaborate backstory or justification to calm me down. Last year, at a dinner party, I publicly shuddered at the idea of multiple births after the subject of quadruplets was broached. Silence descended as people fiddled with their silverware. I learned later to my intense mortification that a couple at the far end of the table recently had had triplets.

"They've probably heard that reaction before," said Dinah soothingly when I told her what I had blurted. "Triplets are unimaginable for a lot of people, particularly for you, because you don't have kids. And that couple should have spoken up and said, 'We have triplets, I know it sounds like a lot of work, but it's rewarded us a hundred times over,' or, you know, something trite like that. Instead of making everyone squirm because they knew something you didn't."

Tom's response was more succinct. It usually was. I could relay the most complex, baroque problem to him, and his response will be seven words or less. Stock answers include *So stop doing it, then; Well, that's his problem; Just tell her no;* and *Why do you care?* It's freeing, in a way.

Addressing my multiple-births blunder, he said, "Sometimes you should think before you speak." As much as I resented his remark, he was right. So many people are undergoing IVF these days that a lone baby is passé. Who *doesn't* have a litter of infants?

"How about that woman who talked about her nephew for forty-five minutes?" I fumed. "I never met her nephew, so is it too much to ask that he should at least be interesting? An investment banker who snowboards is not compelling to me. Then she took out photos of his kids."

"You should have moved on to someone else," Tom observed mildly.

It was more satisfying to vent to Julie, whose horror of social gatherings, particularly those that take place past 3 P.M., matches my own. "When I go to parties, all I ever do is calculate how soon I can leave," she once told me. If she and her husband, Paul, find themselves attending a party at a friend's apartment, "we walk to the door and as we're buzzing to be let in, we want to say into the speaker, 'We have to leave soon.'"

Maybe if I had chosen a different vocation—if I was a police officer, say, or a teacher—I would at least have been forced to deal more effectively with the outside world. Instead, I'll go on a writing jag and the days will slip past so that when I eventually emerge from my apartment, blinking, I'll wince at my reflection in the plate-glass window of a store. Most of the time I have Car Face, the gray, puffy-eyed, slack-mouthed look you get when you've been on a long road trip and finally lurch stiff-legged out of your vehicle at a gas station.

And the longer I stay walled up, the more emotionally fragile I am when I creep out of my abode. And so as I attempt to go to the drugstore or the dry cleaner like a normal person, I must ensure that my mood stays serenely level, or I deteriorate rapidly.

Recently Tom was walking with me to our neighborhood pizza place after I had holed up inside for the entire weekend, and I saw him scan my face anxiously when we both spotted the crumpled body of a sparrow on the sidewalk.

"Don't be weird," he pleaded. This is perhaps the number one thing he says to me.

"Did you see that poor little crushed bird," I whispered in a ghostly monotone, eyes downcast. *All is death, death and decay.*

"Let's just get some pizza," he said desperately. "Pepperoni? Hmm? How about onions?"

"I hope it wasn't tortured to death by kids in the neighborhood."

"Have you ever seen the kids in our neighborhood torture anything? It probably got hit by a car and died before it knew what was happening."

"I suppose so," I murmured.

Recently I decided to make a break out of Cuckoo Town and go out for the entire day, like a functional human, rather than a skinless chicken breast wrapped in cellophane. And so I began in the morning, full of optimism. I actually like walking around my neighborhood, which was settled in the early part of the last century by Italian immigrants. Their descendants still display statues of the Virgin Mary in the modest front yards of their apartments.

I eased into the day with a visit to one of my favorite stores, an old-time purveyor of underwear, housecoats, and "dungarees" run by two elderly brothers who are an institution in the neighborhood. Merchandise is arranged inside wooden shelves that line the walls, as it has been for a half-century (you describe what you want and they root through the drawers), and purchases are rung up on an ancient cash register. All day long a steady trickle of loyal customers stop inside the narrow shop (if the patrons number three or more, one brother throws his hands up and cries "It's nuts in here!").

I've often bought things that weren't strictly necessary because I loved talking to the brothers, who started working in the store right after World War II. This time I purchased yet another package of white sport socks for Tom to add to the teetering pile I had already gotten him. "How's business?" I asked.

"Good, good," the more garrulous brother said. The other was standing at the counter, hunched over the sports section of the *New York Post.* "Lotta housecoats. People come in, they buy eight, ten at a time before they go to It-ly to take them to all their relatives."

I looked behind me at the row of brightly colored housecoats. "Eight dollars apiece seems like a bargain to me," I said. "You could probably jack that up a little, don't you think?"

He waved his gnarly hands. "No! No. We like to keep the price low." He darted over to the housecoats and fluffed some of them out for display. "Almost time to switch over to flannel housecoats," he muttered. "Cold weather coming." He examined a label inside a blue checked number. "Made in China," he said. "Nothing made in the USA no more." Then he moved on to a pile of Lee jeans, which he neatly refolded. "I started working here right after World War II," he said. He says this every time. "People tell me I should retire. What am I gonna do all day? I like to work, talk to people."

Prompted by my questions, he started reminiscing about the old neighborhood, once the province of dockworkers and sailors who worked in the nearby Brooklyn Navy Yard before it closed down in the sixties. "Lotta those sailors were Norwegian," he told me. "They went to all the bars around here. Used to be a lot more bars. And a few blocks away there was a rest-a-rant, like a Scandinavian lunch place, where they used to eat." He looked at his brother, who was still bent over the paper. "You remember that?" The brother nodded.

Then he moved on to another favorite subject, the future of the shop. His son, a fireman, and daughter, a teacher, have told him that they will not take over the business. "I'm probably the last one," he said. "I don't know what's going to happen. Sixty years I been in business. I guess the place'll close up." *Uh-oh. Here comes the rain again.* I moved quickly to hand him my money and escape before my mood slid downward.

I stepped out into the sunshine. *See? This is fun,* I told myself. I especially loved my neighborhood in the morning, when the shopkeepers swept the streets in front of their stores and gossiped with one another. And how could I properly call myself a writer unless I got out there and eavesdropped on the world, which is what writers do best?

I passed a coffee shop where I had overheard many an intriguing conversation. Just last week, Tom and I had stopped in for coffee and a sticky bun. Sitting at the booth behind us was the resident coffee-shop hang-about, a wiry guy in his fifties named Eddie with scraggly reddish hair and a bandanna around his neck. From what Tom and I had gathered over the years, Eddie appeared to run some sort of Internet company out of his home but was forever nursing a coffee inside the shop and talking to the employees, who treated him with tolerant good humor. "Hey," he yelled to a waitress who rushed by with a pot of coffee, "this song that's playing. It's the Vapors, right? I remember this song. Shit, I might have seen them in concert." But his patter had a nervous edge to it, and he seemed even more fidgety than usual. Every time the shop door opened, he looked up warily.

After a few minutes, a young couple came in and silently took a seat next to him. The younger man ordered a coffee, regarded his scraggly booth-mate, and cleared his throat. "You know why I had to fire you, right?" he said. Tom nudged me. Something was about to go down.

"No," said Eddie. "No, I don't. And you didn't even call me to tell me why. You didn't have the decency."

"Yes, but I texted you. Listen, there are a number of reasons why this isn't working out. First of all, the cat likes to eat in the morning, and we know you're not a morning guy."

"Shit. I've been there at eleven-thirty, eleven forty-five. That's still morning."

Tom and I had grown adept at pretending to talk to each other when we were spying on people, using nods and gestures like extras in a play. Today we had the distinct privilege of watching a cat-sitter firing in progress. They should have known better than to hire that guy.

The woman broke in. "And we feel"— she glanced at her husband for encouragement—"we feel that you didn't come every day, either."

"What? Of course I did." He widened his eyes.

Lying, I mouthed to Tom.

"We measured the cat food. There was no way."

Eddie distractedly rubbed a calloused hand over his face. "You measured the cat food? Jesus."

The younger guy nodded. "It wasn't just that. Why were our pillows from the bed on the couch? I mean, look, it's fine if you hang out, but—"

Eddie was indignant. "I was playing with the cat! I was lying down on the couch with the cat, giving it quality time, like you told me to do!"

The younger guy shook his head. "We just had to get someone else." Eddie said nothing and looked bleakly out the window. "Listen," the guy went on. "Do you want to be considered a reserve cat sitter?"

After a moment, Eddie pulled himself together. "Yeah," he said finally. "Yeah. That would be cool."

Today I bypassed the coffee shop—too much to do. Then I walked by a church with a hand-lettered sign taped on the front door. BAKE SALE INSIDE FOR CHILDREN'S CHARITIES, it read. What heartless monster could continue walking? I went in. Four card tables were piled with goods. I scrutinized the selections carefully, passing over the sexier items—the chocolate chip cookies, Rice Krispie treats, and neatly frosted chocolate cupcakes—to find what I wanted. On the third table sat a crooked, grayish Bundt cake of indeterminate flavor with a swampy surface, as if it hadn't been baked enough. A too-thick layer of red-sugar sprinkles had been dumped over the wetness like sawdust over a stain. The crimson dye had oozed out of the sprinkles so that it looked like the cake had been stabbed and was bleeding.

"I'll take it," I said to the lady who was watching me expectantly. I picked up a bag of dark, lumpy shot puts that might have been burned oatmeal cookies. "These, too."

The woman beamed. "Wonderful!" I beamed back. My small good deed buoyed me. So far, all was well.

Every time I find a community group or an elementary school holding a bake sale, I stop in, carefully choose the most unappetizing items, and buy them. I can't tolerate the thought of some well-meaning person spending an afternoon making a hideous Bundt cake that no one will touch. At least a few of the frosted brownies are going to go, but those fruitcake cookies? If I don't buy them, I will be haunted by the scene of a grim-faced parishioner or parent of a first grader sadly throwing out her stale, forlorn creation at the end of the sale.

Which of course is what I do, too. I take them home (to avoid another scene that torments me, of a dismayed baker who spies his uneaten fruitcake cookies in a nearby trash can), and then I stuff them into my own garbage bin. Tom correctly thinks that I'm insane, and further, that I encourage inept baking, but I can't help it.

In the same vein, I can never resist going into a women's exchange store, one of those humble nonprofits that help women who have fallen on rough times sell their handcrafted doodads. Originally these stores were part of a national movement after the Civil War, which left many women without husbands or a way to earn a living. The storefront displays of these places will *tear your freakin' heart out:* hand-knit sweaters and crocheted napkins and pastel baby clothes. What cretin, what inhuman ogre could walk past that sock monkey sitting hopefully in the window, waiting to be taken home? I once spent two hundred dollars at the Baltimore Woman's Industrial Exchange, and did I need that mint-green knit afghan, the set of woven potholders? I also stop at all lemonade stands offering room-temperature beverages that are probably half saliva, or urine. I stop at any farm stand with a trusting coffee can on a table to stuff your money in and buy ten squashes that end up rotting on my kitchen counter.

And so, clutching my lumpy, wet, cellophane-wrapped Bundt cake, I continued on. *Yes, all is well,* I told myself. I thought of a popular British wartime poster that crisply instructed the citizenry, KEEP CALM AND CARRY ON. That would be my new motto.

But then I was rattled by a series of annoying encounters. As I went to the gym, I opened the door for a woman who didn't thank me—or even look at me. I noticed that the guy who loudly and repeatedly blew his nose into the neckline of his shirt as he clomped on the running machine was there, so I moved as far from him as I could. Then, as I climbed onto an elliptical machine, I realized I had forgotten my iPod to block out the loud dance music my gym plays. I am part of the tiny minority who prefer what a friend of mine calls Contractor Rock, which is the J. Geils and Billy Squier that your contractor plays to keep his energy up as he rips open your walls.

And so I was forced to listen as a guy behind me with a backward baseball cap ignored the NO CELL PHONES sign and dialed up his bud.

"Dude," he brayed. "S'going on? Not much. Chillin,' chillin.' You? What's up? Yeah, me neither. So what's happening?"

This fruitless search for something that was "up" went on for twenty minutes. A glare in his direction was all I could muster. I'm always afraid that if I confront someone, he's going to flip out and cause a scene, or stab me. And so I fume silently, and then for the next hour I try out various snappy retorts. *Hey there, sorry to interrupt your chillin,' but do you mind turning off your phone, like the sign plainly says?*

As I left the gym for the grocery store, I dialed my friend Lou. "I really have to try not to let rude people get to me," I said.

"Tell me about it," said Lou, who could handily access his latent rage at any time. He ticked off his pet peeves. "I hate when girls go to stretch out on the mats and then lie down and proceed to text. They'll do one halfhearted sit-up, and then check if they got a response. They aren't stretching anything except their *thumbs.* Then they have to have the frequent sips of water because just the thought of working out has *dehydrated* them! Nothing's happened yet, but they're drinking! Take a sip, adjust hair, take a sip, adjust hair."

Lou was now fully cranked. "How about people who warm up for the treadmill by putting the sole of their foot to the back of their head? Why? Oh, and don't forget the other stretch that involves craning the neck constantly to see who else is in the gym!"

"I know, but I—"

"What about clappers who watch sporting events and feel the need to vocalize every goal or score? Imagine if everyone who watched *Family Feud* did that! What are they so excited about? Are they part owners? Do they have a bet riding on it?"

Unfortunately Lou was not helping my mood. I hung up and

journeyed onward to the bank. I passed a guy standing on the sidewalk with no discernible purpose. "Hey, there," he said. "Smile!" I glowered at him. Why do men like to tell women to smile? Am I in a pageant? Who walks down the street smiling?

My phone rang. It was my mother. "I just watched the best show, *e-vah*," she enthused. "You've got to tape it. It's called *Real Sports with Bryant Gumbel.* Now, I generally hate watching sports, especially golf, which I can't even bear to hear your father discuss. But you know, this show goes deep into the lives of some of these sports figures, and . . ."

I was surprised that my mother was proselytizing about one of her "programs." Usually this was my father's domain. Once a week I would receive a call from him about the joys of CBS's *Sunday Morning* ("You learn so much, and a lot of the segments are very uplifting"), *Battlestar Galactica* ("pure escapism"), and *The Shield* ("real quality writing, just so many great characters, the show ended but it's available on DVD").

". . . reporters profile their personalities," my mother was saying, "and a lot of these football players give their time and money to these incredible causes, it's just very inspiring." Then she stopped. "What's wrong?" she said suddenly. "You sound upset."

"No, I'm not. I just feel defeated sometimes when I leave the house. People can be so irritating."

"You're just focusing on the bad ones. Most people mean well. It's silly to fixate on the rude ones, and a waste of energy, because it's really the other person's problem. There's no way you're going to change people, so why not let it go? Honest to Pete, that's what I love about getting older. I don't focus so much on other people."

"You have gotten mellower," I allowed. "So how would you have handled this one? I was just at the seafood market and the couple behind me was making out furiously and it was just the three of us in the store. I don't quite know why the smell of dead fish got them going. Should I have said something?"

"Nah. A confrontation isn't worth it most of the time. It upsets you more than them, and then you'd chew on it for days. Anyway, they were getting off doing that in public, so they probably would have loved a reaction. Let it go."

"I just feel like people were more polite with each other back in the day."

She snorted. "That's because they were. I was there. I think a lot of it changed when parents began thinking that their children were entitled, like in school when kids started being allowed to talk back to teachers. But listen: This is now. Stop fixating. After you hang up, just start counting the good encounters you have with people. I think you'll probably be surprised. And talk to people. The world is smaller and friendlier when you engage. It just is. What does Tom always tell you?"

I sighed. "'Don't be weird.'"

"Right." She told me about her recent encounter with a woman in a coffee shop who stood next to her at the milk-and-sugar station. My mother was intimidated because she was tall, chicly dressed, and elegantly coiffed. "I thought, *This is not going to be a nice person*, but I said, 'I'm sorry I'm in your way, but my coffee has to be the exact color I like, or I can't drink it.' Well, she was so nice, and said she couldn't let her husband fix her coffee because it had to have the exact amount of sugar and cream in it or she'd pour it out. I shouldn't have made assumptions about her, and I see you do that a lot—judging people. You write their story for them before they've had a chance to open their mouths."

I told her I would try to stop, even as I doubted that the strangers in my neighborhood were quite as friendly as the ones in her small suburban town. I was proved right on my final errand when a scantily clad girl with a blond pixie cut shoved ahead of me on the sidewalk so that I stumbled onto the street. I scowled at her back. *Could your shorts be any shorter?* I ranted in my head. *Why give everyone a free show? Nice tiny tube top so your stupid back tattoo is visible. You're hip! We get it!*

I got closer to her and realized she had headphones on, so she hadn't been aware of me on the sidewalk. Then I got even closer and got a gander of her tattoo. It was festooned with tiny hearts and flowers. NANA, it said.

13

His 'n' Hers Tiger-Print Underwear
in Soft, Shape-Retaining Fabric

I spent many, many hours as a youth lying on my bed, sequestered from all that fresh air and sunshine, paging through my favorite catalogs. For those of us who grew up in the seventies and eighties, poring over them was a rite of passage. Those portals to a more glamorous, merchandise-filled life were our version of cable television. They fueled my burning desire to be blithely rich, if only to be able to call up Swiss Colony and casually order a Dobosh Torte, a fifteen-layer chocolate cake that seemed the height of sophistication at the time.

I was hypnotized by Swiss Colony's offerings, especially the gargantuan gift boxes overflowing with an explosion of gaily wrapped cheese wedges, petits fours, and vaguely named but enticing "beef logs." *Someday,* I would think. *Someday when I'm a grown-up and I have my own money, I will call this catalog and order whatever I want. Also, I will drive an orange Corvette Sting Ray.*

My friend Julie never gravitated toward foodstuffs, instead

spending *her* youth indoors studying the wares of Lillian Vernon. "The stuff was brightly colored, and more important, it was cheap, so you could actually order things," she says. "Like the roly-poly pens, which were five pens in different rainbow colors with sand in them so they stood up like Weebles. It was all about getting things personalized, too, which is so fun when you're a kid." (Offering monograms for the masses was a canny move on Lillian's part.)

My sister Dinah used to regularly lose herself in the pastel world of Avon. "Avon rarely had a light touch when they made up their models," she says. "Usually they would be wearing three or four different colors of eye shadow. Their lids looked like peacock feathers. They were obviously going somewhere glamorous, somewhere middle school kids were not invited. That's where I wanted to be."

One of my favorite things about Avon was its tradition of bestowing on its perfumes nuttily exotic names, from the now-discontinued Far Away Fantasy, To a Wild Rose, and Lemon Velvet to one of its more current men's fragrances, the not-so-evocatively-titled Perceive. Perceive? But I, too, daydreamed over the Avon catalog. What I really wanted to order was the carefree self-confidence of the fresh-faced models. High school is about never being quite right, and in the catalog world, nobody looked awkward. Those pink-cheeked models appeared to take all of that shiny merchandise for granted, in a way that I never would.

I grew up, as George Orwell once put it, "lower upper-middle class." My father was a JC Penney manager in a town of doctors and lawyers. While I was well aware that I had it leagues better than most people in the rest of the world, my folks were constantly battling debt in their (ultimately futile) quest to remain in that comfortable town. If they bought us something, it was not replaced unless it physically fell apart. For twenty-two years, I had the same foam pillow on my bed, which gradually compressed into a hard rectangle with the texture of a dentist's lead blanket for X-rays. That pillow, along with my rigid secondhand mattress, which was as flat as a Japanese tatami mat, ensured that I didn't get a decent sleep for decades. But it would never have occurred to me to ask for another.

I yearned, with rampant teen shallowness, to live like our glamorous neighbors, the Roses. I babysat their children and frequently brought along my sister Heather to help (and, continuing the family tradition of parsimony, gave her one sixteenth of my fee for the privilege). When we had bundled the kids off to bed, Heather and I would nose around their spotless home and marvel at their offhand affluence.

"Look at this," Heather would say, opening the fridge to reveal a silver bowl of whipped cream and another of strawberries. "Real whipped cream! No can! They must put it on the strawberries for dessert. On a Tuesday night!" She held up a box. "And look. Godiva mints. Not for company. Just *for eating*." She darted to the kitchen sink. "Did you see this?" She held up a container of dishwashing liquid. "They don't water down their dish soap like Dad does. Look at how thick it is!"

In my fevered mind, those people in the catalogs lived like the Roses, airbrushed to perfection and surrounded by all of their accessories for the Good Life. I just knew that if I possessed the right stuff, all of my insecurities would melt away. Which is why catalogs were the ideal fantasy fodder. If I were to go to the mall and glimpse some of that merchandise up close, the strange colors and hanging threads would be disappointingly apparent (and seeing the clothes on my lumpy teen body was inevitably worse). But not with catalogs, whose transformative possibilities waited enticingly, and conveniently, in the future.

Perhaps unsurprisingly, my most-thumbed catalog was

JC Penney, because with my father's employee discount and falcon eye for sales, there was a small chance that we might actually be able to buy something. The Christmas catalog sent me into paroxysms of greed. I burned for that kid-sized cardboard pop-up house and the doll that came with a trunkful of a dozen outfits. Quantity, not quality, was crucial. What fun was the Baby Alive doll, which "ate" real fruit-colored food that ended up in a viscous yellow or orange splotch in her diapers, unless it came with three thousand refill packages of baby food?

Heather would stare, year in, year out, at a grainy photo in the Penney's catalog of the Easy-Bake oven and its accompanying mixes. "To this day, I would just die to receive that in the mail," she says in hushed tones. "There was the regular assortment, the deluxe, and the mega-deluxe. You know which one I wanted. And I never forgot the child-sized electric cars, which back in the day were so foreign and magical. You'd fantasize about being the only one driving it around in your neighborhood."

That our parents would bark with laughter if we asked for these items only made the longing worse. When I was nine, I ventured into the living room where my mother was reading the newspaper after work. I hesitantly asked if she would buy me the Easy-Bake oven from the catalog, making what I thought was an exceedingly generous offer to share it equally with my sisters.

"Sure, sweetheart," she said absently, her eyes still on the arts section.

Hope and suspicion wrestled within me. Was this a trick? Had I caught her in a magnanimous mood? Then she looked up and I knew.

"I'll just tell your father to work seven days a week instead of six," she said with freezing calm. "No problem! And I'll put in for more overtime, because I only worked three nights this week." I slowly backed out of the room.

Happily, deprivation powered my creative mind. I may well have become a writer because of the fantasies I conjured of a new, improved me living in a stately pleasure dome. Guests would marvel at the artistic verve of my foot-shaped shag rug, the sheer, wasteful luxury of my giant baseball-glove-shaped chair and my tabletop air-hockey game.

It's been a few decades since I read every page of a Penney's catalog, but I was afforded the opportunity not long ago when I gave a book reading at a church in Fairfield, Connecticut. My folks, as they often do, loyally showed up, and afterward, the organizers thoughtfully presented us with some vintage Penney's catalogs they had procured on eBay.

The next day I leafed through a dusty 1975 edition, chuckling at the his 'n' her overall sets, the tiny polyester light-blue leisure suits for incredibly bummed-out boys, the Evel Knievel Daredevil Action stunt cycle.

When I got to page 163, I stopped laughing. What was this? For $19.95, you could buy your very own JC Penney ceramic water pipe. "For a cooler, smoother smoking experience," read the caption. "Can be smoked by 1, 2, or 3 persons at a time." They didn't even bother with a perfunctory "for tobacco use only" warning at the bottom. They knew. They knew.

I dialed up my father. "Dad? Did you know your company's catalog used to sell water pipes?"

"Well, no, that's not true," he said. "We didn't do plumbing parts. Automotive, yes, but, I don't recall any—"

I interrupted him. "You smoke pot with a water pipe. It makes the smoke more mellow. Apparently."

"I find that hard to believe. Are you sure?"

I informed him that I most certainly was, hung up the phone, and examined the catalog more closely. Oh my. On page 304 was a Glenfield 60 *semiautomatic rifle* ("Save $8.00!"). Well, at least it wasn't offered in the Christmas catalog. And here we have some skimpy, 100 percent nylon tricot His 'n' Hers Tiger-Print Underwear, in—*gaack*—"soft, shape-retaining fabric." Why would you want your nylon tricot to *stay molded in the shape of your private parts*? Had my parents bounded down the stairs for breakfast in those getups, I would have headed straight to the therapist's couch before preschool. Over in the housewares section, a black fake-fur bedspread that would have shamed Hugh Hefner was on offer, with matching black fake-fur draperies. Missing was the warning not to light up a postcoital cigarette around all of that spun acrylic, unless you wanted your new bedroom to be a burn unit.

My head swam as I kept flipping the pages in alarm. The entire catalog was a louche countercultural *carnaval* of sleaze: blacklight posters, a child's T-shirt with the sweet, endearing slogan DO IT IN THE DIRT, a doll called Growing Up Skipper ("Turn her arm and she grows a full ½ inch," meaning that a large pair of jugs erupts through her chest cavity). Even the straight-laced automotive section peddled floor mats for the car embossed with a dazed, grinning bear and the saying IF IT FEELS GOOD, DO IT! (Tell me: What activity pops into your head? Right. Me, too.)

And my father willingly brought this filth into our home? Even the cardboard walk-in playhouses I once coveted evinced a bleakness my younger eyes had missed. I had always yearned for the Burger King Playhouse, a cardboard drive-through window that seemed festive at the time, with its plastic burgers and crisp paper hats for the workers. When I studied the catalog photo with older, wearier eyes, I saw a chubby kid, already a victim of supersizing, sitting inside the window, hunched over a Burger King bag that he's about to hand off to a "customer." It's the single most depressing toy I've ever seen. *Hang on for a few years, kid, and your "dreams" can come true!*

But by far the most disheartening toy that JC Penney offered in 1975 was the Sunshine Valley House, a pop-up vinyl abode that housed the free-livin,' free-lovin' Sunshine family. There was groovy, long-haired patriarch Steve, granny-dress-and-sandals-wearing Stephie (his girlfriend, presumably, because they certainly didn't need a piece of paper to tell the world how they felt), and tiny, illegitimate Baby Sweets. An extra $3.87 bought you a Family Activity Craft Pack, including the unsettling River Trip Pack, complete with miniature frying pans for "live-off-the-land" suppers. The whole sordid drama unfolded in my adult mind. Too bad for Baby Sweets that the river trip was a one-way journey, after Steve couldn't pay the bills with free love and had to sell the pop-up house. *It won't be so bad, living by the river,* Stephie thinks. *At least we all have each other. Maybe another baby will bring us closer. I won't tell Steve I'm throwing away my diaphragm. It'll be a surprise!*

After I made my upsetting discovery I brought the musty catalog to my folks' house and made my father look through it. "You see?" I demanded. "Sodom and Gomorrah."

But my father was absorbed in the men's pajamas. "Boy, I remember that robe," he said dreamily. "Had it for years. Never frayed."

"Dad," I said. "Look here." I pointed to a page that peddled a red fake-fur toilet-seat cover, which offered both comfort and the convenient ability to absorb pesky stray drips. "When did you start catering to pimps?"

"Well, we were reflecting the demands of the customers at the time," he faltered, but then he cracked and burst out laughing. (Later he forwarded jpegs of some of the choicer items to his Penney's cronies, who also had a good chortle.)

I loved to rib my father, but I knew everything is different seen through kids' eyes. What princess canopy bed could possibly match the hype of my overheated dreams? Who among us has not been crushed when those long-awaited Sea-Monkeys arrived, and they weren't wearing crowns and smiling but were tiny brine shrimp that resembled waterlogged silverfish? I thought back to the time when I finally procured a credit card during the summer of my first year of college and, coached by Dinah and Heather in the background, ordered a small gift box from Swiss Colony.

Every day we ran for the UPS man. When the package arrived, we tore it open.

The shriveled petits fours from the gift box were the size of sugar cubes. "Jeez," said Dinah. "They looked huge in the catalog." She took a cautious sniff. (We Dunns like to sniff our food first, like forest animals.) "It smells a little like air freshener." She took a bite. "Yuck," she declared, and pushed it away.

The Dobosh Torte was similarly tiny, as well as waxy, dry, and tasteless. "I can't eat this thing," said Heather, spitting it out with a gagging noise.

"We never should have ordered this stuff," I said, tossing the whole mess into the trash.

Heather folded her arms. "Next time we order from Harry & David."

Of course, the goods from Harry & David's were just as disappointing. It took a lot of credit card debt for me to realize how often the product would never live up to my wild expectations. So after many similar letdowns (and being consumed by guilt over wasted paper) I have whittled down my catalogs to exactly one: the Vermont Country Store. Known as "Purveyors of the Practical & Hard-to-Find," the Vermont Country Store was established in 1946 and is a general celebration of the Good Old Days, Before Everything Got S'Darn Complicated. It's possibly the world's least sexy catalog (and once you're on their mailing list, brace for an influx of medical-footwear catalogs that sell therapeutic socks and allow you the depressing option of "Shopping by Condition"). But I eagerly flip through its pages, glorying in resurrected products such as the pink Princess phone, the Bermuda bag, chocolate cream drops, and packs of handkerchiefs.

The buzzwords here are *comfort* and *dependability*, and most of the upbeat catalog copy that accompanies the old-fashioned line drawings emphasizes these qualities. The goods are divided into sections such as Household & Cleaning, Footwear, and Tried & True, but I think more apt categories would be *I'd Like to Know Why Everyone Is in Such an All-Fired Hurry All the Time* ("Manual Olivetti typewriter types at a pace you can think"). Or *Why Should I Throw Away My Money on a New Gadget That Will Break in a Month?* ("Remember the Fuller Brush man? He's still making quality cotton mops.")

Tried & True would be better described as *Marion? Where Are My Reading Glasses, I Can't See the Blasted Numbers on This Goddamn Thing.* ("End remote rage! Extra-large, easy-to-use, lighted big-button remote control—what could be simpler?") The bespoke toy section should be the more expansively titled *In My Day, Kids Could Be Kids, and They for Darn Sure Didn't Need a Pile of Electronic Gewgaws to Have Fun* (Original Lincoln Logs with 115 Wooden Pieces—"building houses and memories that last"). And the food emporium should be headed *I'd Like to Eat Something I Can Identify, Thanks, So You Can Keep Your Parmesan Foam and Your Fusion Food* ("Whirley Pop makes popcorn that tastes the way it was meant to").

My very favorite section is Apothecary (an obsession I share with many beauty editors and bloggers). It's like looking through your bathroom cabinet's old yearbook. Tigress perfume, with the animal-print bottle cap! Indian Earth, in the tiny clay pot, which imparts a "sun-kissed" nuclear orange glow! Bonne Bell Ten-O-Six zit vanquisher! And, not one, but *four* Memory Lane shampoos—"Gee, Your Hair Smells Terrific," LemonUp, Body on Tap (made from beer), and—are you ready?—Psssssst spray-on dry shampoo. Freakin' Psssssst! (Yes, the name was that long, a tribute to seventies excess.)

But as tempted as I have been to ransack the Apothecary for some LemonUp, or perhaps Ondine Eau de Parfum, a resurrected 1954 scent with the daring slogan "Don't wear Ondine unless you mean it," I have learned to control myself. Having waved good-bye to the naïve excitement of my youth, I now buy items that are strictly practical. Although I must admit that when my latest package arrived from Vermont, my reaction was a little disturbing.

"Oh good!" I cried to Tom. "My wool socks are here, and my egg separator!" Then I tore open that box as if it contained an Easy-Bake oven with mega-deluxe accessories.

14

You Make Me Feel Like Dancing

Julie phones at 9:07 A.M., as she does every day on her journey to the gym.

JULIE: I'm very prepared for working out today, because I just added a bunch of new songs to my iPod.

JANCEE: You know what? If anyone ever looked at the lineup on my iPod, it's one hundred percent embarrassing. I could probably count on one hand the number of songs I could display publicly. My entire collection consists of songs that, if you're playing them in a car, you have to turn down when you get to a stoplight and other people can hear you.

JULIE: Oh, please. Me, too.

JANCEE: I know one person who goes to my gym, and just in case I run into him, I have a Jesus & Mary Chain tune that I can quickly put on. The rest of the time I'm taking out my earbuds a lot and nervously checking them, because I'm sure that everyone can hear the Scritti Politti song that's blasting. Don't you feel like everyone is listening to something new and hip on their iPods except for you?

JULIE: Yes, because they are. Sometimes when someone is on the rowing machine next to me, I quickly put on En Vogue's "Free Your Mind" to replace Glen Campbell's "Wichita Lineman."

JANCEE: Listen, when I worked at *Rolling Stone,* one of the questions I used to pull out to ask musicians was "What is the perfect pop song?" They always loved to answer that one. And no less than Nirvana producer Butch Vig said "Wichita Lineman." So you're cooler than you think.

JULIE: If you say "perfect pop song" to me and I don't think about it, the song that pops into my head is "Tell Her About It" by Billy Joel. Although I wouldn't want it on my iPod.

JANCEE: Soon we won't care at all if anyone sees what we're playing, and that's when we'll know we're officially old. Although we're on our way with our musical choices. For instance I downloaded "I'm Your Man" last week, and—

JULIE: The Leonard Cohen song? But that's hip.

JANCEE: No, the one by Wham! Okay? What's odd is that when this song came out in the eighties, I wouldn't have been caught dead buying a Wham! album. I mean, I never bought pop. I would never have deigned to buy something by Hall and Oates, yet now I find myself downloading "One on One." You know, there's a theory floating around that every single iPod has at least one Hall and Oates tune on it.

JULIE: I believe it.

JANCEE: I think I'm rebelling or something from so many years of working at *Rolling Stone* and MTV and being musically correct.

JULIE: There's a section on iTunes called the Genius Sidebar, which recommends songs to you based on what you've gotten already. And I swear to God, the Genius Sidebar (*whispers*) knows me better than I know myself.

Let me just tell you what I'm buying. I like the heavy-metal ballads—"Home Sweet Home" by Mötley Crüe, "Sometimes She Cries" by Warrant, Winger's "Headed for a Heartbreak"—all that stuff. And they suggested "Fly to the Angels" by Slaughter. They know. They *know*.

JANCEE: (*male voice talking in background*) Tom just walked into the room and said, "What's that thing on your forehead?"

JULIE: Aww. So sweet.

JANCEE: I have a blemish above my eyebrow that is perhaps a little 3-D. But what's good about Tom is that he doesn't notice any change in my appearance whatsoever unless it's some sort of health-related problem, like the giant swelling on my forehead. Otherwise it just doesn't register. I could be wearing nothing but scuba flippers. Which is kind of how I normally dress.

Anyway, I just downloaded the song "Lady (You Bring Me

Up)" by the Commodores. Have you ever seen the video for that one, by the way?

JULIE: Not that I can remember.

JANCEE: I suggest you YouTube it immediately. The Commodores are all gathered in a soccer field to play a game, and they all have these fabulous beards and giant square glasses, except Lionel Ritchie, who has a mustache-and-Afro-mullet combo. And they're all wearing extremely tiny soccer shorts, because in between singing, they play a soccer game against what appear to be braless porn actresses. A classic. But I listened to the song twice and then got bored.

JULIE: That happens a lot. I have a couple of those songs where I got them, listened once, and decided I never wanted to hear them again. Like Leo Sayer's "You Make Me Feel Like Dancing." I listened once and thought, *Okay, ninety-nine cents, I'll take that, sure.* And now every time it comes on, I fast-forward it. So many stupid songs on there. I think that our lists are probably equally bad. Let's have a contest to see who has the worst song. Okay, let me look. I think mine is "The Captain of Her Heart" by Double. Terrible.

JANCEE: I can top it. "(Can't Live Without Your) Love and Affection" by Nelson. Nelson, Jul!

JULIE: I see Nelson and raise you Orleans, "Dance with Me."

JANCEE: "S.O.S." by Abba. They sound especially Swedish on it, like they're barely hanging on to the English.

JULIE: I just downloaded a song by a band called Alter Bridge. You never heard of them. The song is always on VH1. Alter Bridge does a music video and they show all these bad clips from *Celebrity Rehab,* like Tawny Kitaen having a meltdown. So you're listening to this song while Jeff Conaway is sobbing in a wheelchair. Somehow, I had to have it.

JANCEE: Okay, now I'm looking at the Genius Sidebar on my computer and I see that it's recommending "Caribbean Queen" by Billy Ocean. So that will give you an idea of the caliber of songs I'm buying.

JULIE: I saw someone dead again today before I dropped Violet off at school. This time it was Jerry Orbach from *Law & Order.*

JANCEE: That happens to you a lot. But there is a certain sort of civilian who does have a Jerry Orbach look.

JULIE: Okay, I'm here.

JANCEE: Enjoy.

15

I Never Knew It Could
Be Like This

Periodically I force myself to unhook my fingers from the door frame, venture out even farther from my immediate neighborhood, and explore an entirely new country. It must be done, or I would be the human equivalent of a cave fish; in my case, it really does build some much-needed character. Traveling to distant climes, away from my cherished network of comforts, is a no-fail way for me to face my many fears, a partial list being people, change, stray dogs, strange new insects that could bite me and bring forth a latent allergy that causes my death, alien viruses for which I have built up no immunities, and trains with indecipherable schedules that deposit you in an unknown country hundreds of miles from your destination before you figure out you're going the wrong way. Hovering malevolently over them all is a fear of dirt and germs.

For the last three years I have had ample opportunity to deal with these neuroses, as Tom has been researching a book that has taken him all over the world and he kindly brought me along. Our trip to China, which took place two years ago, enabled me to confront one of my most pervasive and debilitating fears: heights.

We started the first day of the Beijing leg of our journey as we usually do: rambling for hours with no particular destination. As we strolled through a seven-hundred-year-old, soon-to-be-demolished *hutong* neighborhood, Tom mentioned that he wanted to walk on the Great Wall the next day.

"Sounds good," I said, keeping the doubt out of my voice. Why couldn't we just take a look at it? Why walk on it? But I didn't want to sound like a grandma. He said that if I was game, he had made inquiries online to a certain Mr. Mu, who would drive us the next morning to a less overrun section of the wall a few hours farther than the one most tourists visited. It was a bit more challenging. Was I up for it?

"Sure," I said weakly.

The next day, Mr. Mu drove us for six hours before pulling up to the entrance of the suitably impressive Great Wall (although it's a myth that you can see it from space). It was higher than I thought—about thirty feet tall—and snaked vertiginously over a dizzying series of steep hills crowned with watchtowers.

"Well, good-bye," announced Mr. Mu. "I will see you in five hours." *Wait, what?* Five hours? I reckoned we'd walk around for a little bit, take some pictures, admire the view, and call it a day. Maybe lunch was involved?

"Didn't I tell you?" said Tom. "We're going to walk on the wall for a few hours, and then Mr. Mu will pick us up at a point farther south."

What? What? Mr. Mu got into his car and drove away. Suddenly it was the first day of kindergarten again and my mother had dropped me off on the steps of the school. *Mommy? Mr. Mu?*

We started up the walkway. *You can do this,* I coached myself.

You are standing on one of the most miraculous manmade structures in the world. Your parents dreamed of coming here and likely never will. Get on with it.

I have a fear of heights so debilitating that when I peer over the second-floor balcony of the Short Hills mall, I am seized with heart palpitations. Some people are terrified of clowns, or the number four (tetraphobia), or loud sounds (phonophobia), but I feel that being scared of heights is legitimate. Height has consequences. You can fall and die.

We made our way up a small hill, which led to a tower. I peeked over the side and was immediately sorry as I saw a couple of large rocks break off from the walkway and tumble down the side of the hill, bouncing like my skull would if I leaned too far off the edge.

The second hill was higher. I was surprised to find that most of the wall is actually made up of stairs—ancient, crumbling steps that are often only about twelve inches high, a neverending StairMaster. It was another shock to discover that much of the wall had no protective bits on the side. A cold, wet wind pushed against me. What if I blew off?

The hills grew steeper as I carefully mounted the steps. My hands shook; my nose ran in humiliating rivulets down my shirt. Three towers down. I wondered how many there were to go. Was it better not to know? I finally asked Tom.

"Thirty," was his reply.

Thirty towers.

I started gibbering quietly, mostly a complicated bargaining process with the Lord if He would only spare me.

The next hill was so steep I was using both my hands and feet to haul myself upward, like a rock climber. I moved forward only because I had no choice; hordes of people marched behind us, even in this less touristy part. I kept my eyes firmly ahead of me and dared not look down as I clung like a beetle to the stairs with sweat-slicked hands and the wind whipped my hair into my nose rivulets.

When we reached the next sharply slanting tower, I began hyperventilating and sat heavily down. "I can't do it," I wheezed. "I have to turn around." Shame flooded me. Why couldn't I be one of those unflappable, sunburned Germans I always encounter in my travels—the same ones I saw visiting my own city who breezily took the subway to the South Bronx to look around?

Tom stroked my hair. "I'm sorry," he said gently. "We can't turn around. Mr. Mu is meeting us at the other end, and I have no way of contacting him. It's a five-hour drive. And look"—he pointed to the long, thick line of sightseers twisting down the hill. "You'd have to fight against this."

I started to cry. "I can't do twenty-six more towers," I said between gasps. We began to argue as my rational mind slipped away and hysteria crept in. This was the sort of genuine nightmare I regularly lurched awake from at home. I wanted to remain in that tower and grip the rocks like a barnacle until a rescuing helicopter arrived. "Please," I blubbered.

As I clung to him and begged, causing what was probably a very entertaining scene for the other tourists, an elderly lady with knee braces and forearm crutches determinedly picked her way past me.

We both began to laugh. Christ. If she could do it, I could. I shakily heaved myself up. At the same moment a slight local woman with windburned cheeks appeared from nowhere and offered to guide me. "Yes, yes, sure," I gabbled, grabbing on to her arm. We negotiated a price that was fair, considering I would have happily ripped off my wedding ring and handed it over. Half my size and as sure-footed as a mountain goat, she dragged me along like an unwieldy trash bag for the remainder of the trip. I only wished she was a little bigger so she could heave me over her shoulder in a fireman's carry and I could simply pass out until it was over.

When I saw Mr. Mu waiting for us in the parking lot, it was all I could do not to run over and give him a lap dance. I suppose the whole experience strengthened me, in the way that a hideously broken bone mends to become more robust. At least now I can look out over the second floor of the mall without even blinking.

Our next journey, to Delhi, India, presented an opportunity for me to face another fear: crowds.

I had dreamed of going to India my whole life. On-screen, it always looked so heart-stoppingly vivid in a way New York City never could. So many of my friends had been there, and every one of them swooned as they recalled the trip, using phrases like "life-changing" and "unforgettably magical." The country will get in your blood, they told me solemnly, and compel you to return again and again.

We arrived in the city after a bone-jarring flight and, half-dead, shuffled into a taxi, but when I sniffed the city's spicy, rich air, I quickly revived. "We're really here!" I whispered, and squeezed Tom's arm. A family of four, somehow balanced precariously on one small moped, swooped in front of us, the woman's fuchsia sari flapping and twisting in the breeze. Our heads snapped around as we tried to take in the colors and sounds of the chaotic traffic.

Then we stopped at a streetlight, and suddenly our taxi was mobbed. A crying woman was holding up her listless, miserable baby. A man with two stumps for arms hollered for money. A child no more than four ran over and held on to the handle of the taxi, telling us he would not let go until we gave him some cash. The man began to beat his stumps on the window. *Wham! Wham! Wham!*

I fumbled for my purse, overcome with an impulse familiar to many who travel, of wanting to help and a fear of being besieged. The driver turned around. "Don't give them money," he warned, "or the car will be surrounded and we won't be able to move." The people kept coming. After an eternity the light changed. I made a vow to donate to a local organization when I returned home, but I felt ashamed that I hadn't obeyed a human impulse to help.

The next morning we made our way through the pushing, jostling crowds on Delhi's teeming sidewalks. I thought the press of bodies was hard until we hit Shastri Park and saw the gangs of screaming, scuttling monkeys darting through the greenery. Hindus consider them to be sacred and feed them peanuts and bananas. Hadn't anyone seen *Outbreak*? Delhi was overrun with hungry rhesus monkeys, an estimated ten to twenty thousand of them. When we were there, reports of "marauding monkey gangs" dominated the papers.

I steered clear. When did interacting with playful monkeys become a required tourist activity? How many vacation photos do I have to see of friends' trips to Brazil or Costa Rica or Cambodia with the requisite shot of rogue monkeys crawling on their shoulders and searching for nits in their hair? What is so charming about a pack of monkeys stealing your sunglasses or snatching the ice cream cone that you just paid for and scampering up a tree? Monkeys aren't cuddly. They screech. They bite. They spread mysterious viruses (see "travel fears," above).

It seemed safer on the street, which was thronged with vendors selling vegetables and bread and batteries and underwear.

Everything imaginable took place on that sidewalk. People were bathing, arguing, relieving themselves, sleeping on mats, eating breakfast. A man in an old La-Z-Boy chair was having his impressively long ear hair carefully trimmed by a barber. Another guy was getting a tooth pulled. A third was casually trimming his toenails.

For the first few days, I did a lot of muttering *Get me out of here* under my breath. I truly did not understand what the hoo-ha was all about. But on the fourth night, the magic did kick in for me—inspired by, of all people, one of our ex-presidents. We had gone to dinner (Delhi's food, by the way, was sublime), and at the entrance of the restaurant we saw, for the fourth time, yet another photo of Bill Clinton. Apparently he'd spent a few weeks in India and had hit every restaurant he possibly could. In the photo, Clinton had his arm around the proprietor. Both were grinning broadly, as were the hundred employees surrounding them. Next to it was a snap of Clinton dancing at an Indian wedding that he seemed to have crashed. He was out of breath and laughing. Lord knows the man had his faults, but was there a living person who enjoyed being around others more than he? At the time, he had to contend with leading the Western world. So why was I squandering my time being tense? When you travel, a sense of control is the first thing to go. What was the point of coming all this way if I didn't eagerly leap into everything like our ex-president did?

And so I stopped fixating on the relentless crush of humanity that heaved and undulated around me at all times. Once you realize you cannot do a thing about the crowds, you have no choice but to put reports of stampedes at Hindu temples out of your mind, relax, and enjoy what really is an extraordinary place.

Traveling to other cities usually makes me appreciate the pristine splendor of my obsessively dirt-free home, but this did not happen on our journey to Tokyo. The whole city was so immaculate that it only made me realize how much cleaner I could become.

Everyone who returns from Tokyo raves about the mindbending high-tech kookiness of the city. One prime example is Namjatown, a huge, hallucinatory amusement park housed inside a sprawling indoor mall called Sunshine City in Ikebukuro. The fever dream of Namco, creator of Pac-Man and other arcade games, it's a dizzying funhouse of weirdness, the best part being the food, particularly the dumpling-centered theme park called Ikebukuro Gyoza Stadium, which mimics a bygone Japanese town with a winding street lined by umpteen gyoza shops, each created by a different, vaunted gyoza chef. Afterward, we visited Ice Cream City, an explosion of candy-colored ice cream shops offering hundreds of flavors, including squid, beef tongue, pumpkin, and Indian curry. I had the soy ice cream, while Tom helped himself to a scoop of the cheese.

But even better than Ice Cream City was my room at the new Peninsula Hotel in the Marunouchi district. It is the most thrilling place I have ever been in. You will need to take out a third mortgage to afford it—we saved for a year—but I will never see those sorts of high-tech perks again. It took a good hour to inspect all of the wonders of that room. I raced around like a kid hyped on too much sugar. (Jaded, I'm not. A music publicist for Queen once told me that when Freddie Mercury arrived at a new hotel room, he would jump on the beds. Freddie is my inspiration.)

The room was more thoughtfully intuitive than the most solicitous butler. When the phone (which displays the time and weather in your hometown) rang, the television and radio automatically muted. The bathroom phone, meanwhile, featured a digital filter to blot out any betraying echo indicating that you were conducting business on the bowl. The thermostat, which was next to the wall-panel Internet radio, had a control button to adjust the room's humidity level. I jacked it so high you could have grown orchids in there. Built into the capacious walk-in closet was a nail dryer, just in case your nails were still wet after your spa manicure. Next to the tub was a "spa" button, which automatically dimmed the lights and switched the radio station to calming music as you sank into the bubbles. Heaven! And—why didn't someone think of this sooner?—a fleet of "privacy" buttons, accessible from the bed and, crucially, the john, just in case a staff member knocked at the door while you were indisposed.

But the very best part of that room was the toilet, demurely hidden by discreet frosted-glass panels. When I clapped my eyes on it, a choir of angels sang sweetly in the background. In fact, there is probably some model that actually provides the music of angels for added comfort and relaxation. I approached this marvel of sanitation with humility and awe. It had an automatic open-and-close lid (usually I handle all lids outside my own home with a crumpled tissue, Howard Hughes–style), auto flush, and an air purifier that instantly neutralized odor.

"I never knew it could be like this," I whispered. It was the ultimate fetish object for a clean freak like myself. Situated by the seat—which was heated, of course—was a thrillingly complicated panel of buttons. Front/rear cleanse. Soft cleanse. Oscillating. Pulsating. There was even an adjustable cleansing wand for added control. And after all that specialized washing, a warm-air dryer with five temperature settings gently stirred your nether regions like a sweet spring zephyr.

"I'm going to try a soft cleanse," I whispered. "No, an oscillating soft cleanse, followed by a medium-heat dry."

"Come on," called Tom. "I found a great noodle place in Roppongi."

"Five more minutes!" I called desperately. I did everything but lick that toilet. Which I probably could have.

I wanted to live in that bathroom. For the week of our stay, I practically did. Every night I would guzzle pints of water. Time to go to the bathroom again! Sometimes I would rush toward the toilet to try and beat the automatic lid. It always won. By the end of the week, the toilet and I seemed to have reached an affectionate understanding. If I woke in the night, that toilet knew. Before my feet reached the floor next to my bed, I could swear I heard the discreet *zzzzt* of the lid opening. "You rascal," I said one night with a chuckle.

Tom stirred in the bed. "Who are you talking to?" he asked blearily.

"What? Oh, no one."

At the end of that enchanted week, I had to be physically pried away from my beloved new friend. It was no surprise that when I returned to the States, my cleanliness mania grew alarmingly worse. Toilet paper seemed so barbaric. So maybe not every trip built up my character. In fact I think our jaunt to Japan diminished my character, because I've spent a little too much time since then scheming to buy a top-of-the-line Toto Washlet.

"Don't tell me you're on that toilet website again," Tom said to me this morning as I hunched over my computer.

"Of course not," I said, smoothly changing screens to BBC News. But I can't stop. One day I will possess that toilet, if only to erase the image that haunts me of our final parting, when, for the last time, the lid gently closed, as if it was sadly waving good-bye.

16

This Is a Prank, Right?

Not long ago I was on a flight from New York to Los Angeles and fell into a conversation with my seatmate, a woman in her thirties with spectacular caramel highlights and one of those artfully draped cashmere throws that well-groomed women wear to ward off chilly plane air. Usually I don headphones and whip out a book the minute I sit down, especially after being burned by an incident on my last flight. I had been seated next to a man who, before I had fastened my seat belt securely and adjusted my seat to its upright position, had shaken my hand and boomed, "Good to meet you! How are you today?"

I've logged thousands of hours in the air and have learned that this greeting indicates the dreaded Chatty Person in Sales. The giveaway is the word *today,* followed by repeated usage of your name ("Well, Jancee, I grew up in Chicago but decided to go to school on the East Coast, and you know, Jancee, it's funny . . .").

But this woman—a lawyer for environmental causes, I learned—was low-key and graciously refrained from hogging our joint armrest. And so we traded biographies. I explained that I was joining my husband, who was already in Los Angeles, for a flight to China. Imagine, I went on, that one day your husband tells you he's writing a book and must travel to Tokyo, Delhi, Rome, Mexico City, and Berlin, among other cities, for research and would I like to come along? It had been a dream.

She frowned. "But what did you do with your kids?"

I replied that I didn't have any.

"Why not?" She had already told me that she had two young sons.

This question has been put to me probably a hundred times. It always struck me as an odd thing to ask, because it was so personal, and also the very phrase "Why not?" implied that I was somehow shirking my duty as a woman. In any case, I never seemed to deliver an answer that satisfied my inquisitor. "Well," I began, "my husband and I have always been on the fence about it, and in the meantime, we've been having so much fun that the years have just sort of slipped by." I shrugged.

"Hmm," she said, and I knew what was coming next. "Don't you think it's selfish not to have children?"

This dishearteningly familiar argument never failed to amaze me. Why on earth was refraining from adding a child to a world with an exploding population and diminishing ozone layer selfish?

In the same breath, she switched to fearmongering: Who, she asked me, was going to care for me when I was old?

That one never stirred any alarm, for it always seemed to me that when you reached your dotage, being in possession of a giant pile of money was infinitely more useful than having offspring. A grudging weekly visit or phone call from Junior might be nice, but surely it would be much nicer to be able to afford to rebuff the nursing home in favor of a private nurse and personal chef to care for me in my own cozy surroundings. Cynical? Perhaps. But I always called up the same rosy picture of my doddering years: I am in a down-filled armchair in my expansive library. A fire crackles invitingly in the fireplace as I settle in with a sigh and open a book with my gnarled hand. My private nurse bustles in with a blanket, cooing that she doesn't want me to catch a cold. She tucks it around me as my chef brings me a steaming cup of tea and easy-to-chew, well-buttered toast on a gleaming silver tray. Who needed kids? I'd rather pay staffers to listen to me prattle about the old days than torture some grandchild into listening to creaky tales from my rock-and-roll past. At that point, who would care except my well-paid companions about the time a wobbly Pete Townshend slurred "I love your frock" backstage, lurched to hug me, and knocked me over?

"I don't see being child-free as selfish," I told the woman.

"Well, I can tell you that before I had kids, I was all about me, me, me," she said, fluttering her hand. "Kids really set your priorities straight. Honestly, I never realized how shallow I was before."

Then I got angry. Why was this any of her business? And what was so altruistic about shifting her focus from herself to her kids? "Right," I said, struggling to keep my voice level. "So your decision to reproduce was a selfless act, was it?" (I wasn't quite that articulate, because I was flustered.) "So your motive for having kids was to further the greater good of humanity?"

The rest of the flight was glacially silent.

I probably overreacted. But at that point I was so bone-weary of yet another well-meaning but tactless person joining in the discussion of my sadly empty, tumbleweed-strewn uterus—from the cabdriver who once warned that I'd never be a "real woman" to a grandmotherly type who asked me, with genuine concern, why I "hated children."

Part of my impatience stemmed from my fruitlessly debating the subject with Tom at home. Was there anything worse than two analytical writers on a tediously elliptical loop? We veered endlessly between pro and con. On the one hand, being around children for any length of time made me a bit tense. I'm the person who enters a restaurant, sees shouting kids running in the aisles, and storms out. I deliberately take vacations when school is in session. I gag when I smell chicken nuggets. I flee from noise. Tom's worse. He's like those stern old men in British gentlemen's clubs who glance up sharply when someone rustles a copy of the London *Times* with too much vigor.

On the other hand, what if having a kid was actually fun? At my advanced age, I could only manage to extrude one shrunken, dried-out baby anyway, so it's not as if I would be overwhelmed. So many friends whom I trust have tearfully told me that having children was the best decision they had ever made. Think of life, one of them had said, as if it's a bridge made of rope. The more ropes you have that tether you to the earth, the better. Sometimes I did get the feeling that I was ever so slightly adrift—but maybe everyone felt that way.

And while my weekends with Tom were peaceful idylls filled with books and late breakfasts and old movies, there were times when I felt like our apartment was too ordered, too still. Sometimes—only sometimes—I envied the cheery chaos in the background when I phoned a friend who had kids.

Years passed with no resolution, until we were so tired of the subject that we figured we would simply leave it to fate. I know, I know—sometimes when friends have informed me that a pregnancy "just happened," I have been puzzled. How could a person be so randomly offhand about such an enormous decision? Either you wanted a kid, or you didn't, and if you tossed the birth control pills, surely you were craving a child, if even on an unconscious level.

Yet that is exactly what we decided to do in order to break our crippling deadlock. And as time went by, we both presumed that fate was delivering us a firm no and accepted the fact with equanimity. And at least my advancing age finally managed to halt the flow of family propaganda—the pro-kid presentations, the flow charts and PowerPoint presentations, along with assurances that every family member would babysit for up to a week at a time. Happily, this campaign had dried up along with my womb.

Still, at any familial gathering, someone would make a half-hearted pitch, mostly out of habit. On the previous Labor Day weekend, Tom and I had gone to my folks' place to take advantage of their pool. It was a crumbling old concrete structure that my father was too cheap to heat despite my having bought him a pool heater in desperation, but we were grateful for a place to splash around in nonetheless. On Labor Day, Heather stopped by for a lunch of barbecued pork sandwiches and chocolate pecan bars that my mother had decided to make from her recipe bible, *Southern Living*.

While Tom and Heather's husband, Rob, headed out for a quick game of basketball, we set the table. Then I saw my mother and Heather exchange a brief but significant look.

"So," Heather began, elaborately casual. "I guess you've completely given up on the idea of children, huh?" Heather was always the spokesperson on this topic, and then my mother would unobtrusively chime in. This was a deliberate move. I could just picture my mother telling Heather, *You bring it up. She'll feel pressured if I do it. I saw how irritated she got when I happened to mention that the*

*psychic I consulted last year said I was goin' to have six grandkids, and
I'm only up to four.*

I stopped pouring the iced tea and faced her. "You know what?
I just don't think it's in the cards, and you shouldn't feel bad about
it. I have a life that is more exciting and fun than I ever would
have imagined. Honestly, I don't feel any sort of void."

Heather nodded. "I believe you. I do." My mother hovered behind her, wondering whether she should jump in or not.

"Fate is telling us that it's not happening," I added. "I swear on
my life that I'm all right with it." I grabbed her by the shoulders.
"I'm all right."

My mother, who was pretending to be preoccupied with emp-
tying a bag of potato chips into their "company" cut-glass potato
chip bowl, couldn't resist opening her yap. "But you're not on any
sort of birth control, right, honey?" I hadn't been for five years,
but my mother regularly felt the need to confirm this, apparently
fearful that I was going to tiptoe off to Planned Parenthood behind her back.

"Correct. But at my age, it's highly unlikely that I can produce
even a sickly, three-pound preemie for you at this point. So you
should bug Dinah and Heather for those extra two grandchildren."

Then my mother pointed out, for perhaps the two hundredth
time, that her own mother had been forty-two when she came
into the world. "Mama thought I was—"

"A stomach tumor," I finished.

"So you're not . . . you're not *not* trying."

"Right." I put glasses of iced tea on the table. "Come to
think of it," I said slowly. "Come to think of it, I'm actually a week
late." I waved my hand. "I don't keep track of these things, I just
can't be bothered to write it on the calendar, you know? I just feel
like . . ."

Heather, holding a dripping pickle to place on my parents' company tray, gawped at me. My mother stood motionless, her hand on the silverware drawer. For a moment, all was quiet.

Then they both rocketed forward as I sprang out of the way like a startled frog. "We're going to CVS for a pregnancy test!" Heather shouted to my mother, grabbing her car keys.

Simultaneously my mother scooped up Heather's youngest boy, who had been toddling contentedly on the floor. "I'll take the kid," she said. I saw her retreating back, my nephew's head bobbling over her shoulder as she raced through the house, down the steps of the deck, and toward the sandbox in the backyard. It was all a weirdly choreographed effort, as if it had been rehearsed earlier that day.

Heather drove me to CVS and back at a speed alarming even for a former gum-chewing, permed Jersey girl, then hustled me into the guest bathroom, threw the kit at me, and shut the door.

I took the test and looked around idly while awaiting the results. This bathroom had the distinction of having the world's most uncomfortable shower. It produced only the barest squirt of hot water, and my father had rigged the spigot with a water-saving device, so that you had to stand and wait for enough cold mist to condense onto your body before you could use the soap, an oversized bar the size of a loaf of pumpernickel. My mother had gotten it at a discount store a few years ago, and it never got any smaller. Using it was like rubbing a surfboard all over you, and woe to the bather who drops it on his foot, because . . .

I glanced down at the test.

It was positive.

I gazed at the thing in a daze. *Everything changes from this moment on,* piped a little voice in my head.

A few minutes later I opened the door. "It's positive," I faltered. "I can't believe it."

Heather and my mother clutched each other, screaming and jumping up and down like *The Price Is Right* contestants who have just won the showcase of a trip to Puerto Vallarta, matching Jet Skis, and a years' supply of Turtle Wax. Meanwhile, my reaction was more like the decorous Milwaukee senior who brings a garage-sale vase to *Antiques Roadshow* and is informed that it's Tiffany and worth twenty grand. "Well," these seniors inevitably say with baffling calm. "How about that." It was all just a little too much to absorb.

My mother ran to get the phone. "Call Dinah!" she hollered over her shoulder.

"When are you going to tell Tom?" Heather said, bouncing on her heels. "He has no idea you even took the test!"

"I guess right when he gets back from playing basketball," I said. "Otherwise he'll hear it on the streets. Let's go in the backyard and I'll tell him there." I was still trying to process the news myself but caught their excitement at telling him. *Hey, that's a positive sign,* I told myself. *I'm not upset! I'm eager to tell Tom! That's significant, right?*

Five minutes later Tom returned from the game with Rob, both of them covered in sweat. They were in the midst of laughing about something, but Tom's smile died on his face as I ran over and pulled him to a little table and set of chairs by the pool.

I sat down. "I have something to tell you," I said gravely.

He looked around suspiciously. "What?" he said uneasily. "What?"

"Just have a seat."

His eyes darted to my family, who were clustered by the deck. They were peeking at him, none too discreetly, with big grins.

"What?" Tom said, flapping his arms helplessly. "Do you have a Super Soaker? This is a prank, right?" All of the jokes I had played on my unsuspecting husband conspired to ruin my touching moment, and I had no one to blame but myself.

"It's not a prank," I said soothingly, but he was spooked by the abnormal brightness of my eyes and the sound of Heather shushing my folks.

"What is it?" he said, increasingly distressed. "What is it? Do you have a video camera? Are you filming me?" Suddenly he leapt up and raced blindly toward the house.

I looked over at the group. My father was somberly patting my mother's back. Rob was frowning at a far-off patch of lawn. Heather looked stricken.

They thought I had broken the news and he had run off in terror. I got up and followed him into the house. "Tom," I said quietly, approaching him gingerly, as if he was a bucking bronco. "Listen. I'm pregnant."

He stared at me in shock, then laughed delightedly and hugged me. "That's wonderful," he said, his eyes moistening with tears. I relaxed a little.

As Tom and I drove home to Brooklyn that night, we discovered how incredibly freeing it was to have the pressure of a decision lifted from our shoulders. Cautiously, we began to explore the idea of a new baby and even batted around a few names. To my profound relief, I found that we were a tiny bit . . . could it be that we were a tiny bit excited? I was still plagued by trepidation, but the good thing about pregnancy is that it grants you almost a year to settle in with the idea.

Two months later, after I passed the first round of screenings, Tom ordered up a pile of baby books and we spent one evening paging through them. I started off in a fairly lighthearted mood until I reached a chapter in one book on potential changes to your body.

It seemed that nothing stayed the same on your entire body once a fetus took up residence. Everything morphed, or swelled, or oozed, or turned a different color. I read that I could probably look forward to painful, bleeding, itching hemorrhoids, which often enlarged even further if—no, when—the mother-to-be developed constipation. Other unlucky women found themselves with a condition called a "mask of pregnancy," a yellowish or brownish butterfly-shaped area that could cover the face. *Cover the face?* I kept picturing the movie poster from *The Silence of the Lambs,* Jodie Foster's mouth obscured by an enormous moth. *I'll help you catch him, Clarice.* The litany of potential mishaps continued: skin tags, darkening moles, extra fluid pooling in the feet, which caused them to swell one or even two sizes. So one day you could wake up with a giant pair of new feet?

I grew dizzy as the list of what sounded like semitropical diseases stretched for pages and pages. There was everything but three-foot worms bursting out of your eyes. A dark line that travels down the abdomen, called the linea nigra. Thick hairs in brand-new places. Gourd-shaped, swingy, blue-veined boobs. Increased oil-gland secretion followed closely by an explosion of zits. The leaching of calcium from your bones as the fetus helps itself to your limited supply. Vivid dreaming and nightmares. Softened ligaments (don't make any sudden movements, the book warned, or something could slip or twist!). I pictured myself jerking awake one night from a nightmare and wrenching my softened, calcium-depleted back. Red, itchy palms. Depression.

That last one was already upon me. I hastily phoned my friend Tracy, who had three girls. "When you were pregnant," I asked her, "did you ever get a yellow mask of pregnancy on your face?"

She laughed. "I can't say I did."

"Did your feet go up two sizes?"

"I did go up half a shoe size after my third one was born, yes. But then, think about the joy of having to buy new shoes."

"Skin tags?"

"Okay, yes, I did develop one or two skin tags in strange places, but overall, my skin never looked better. I also have some stretch marks, but they're white and faint at this point. They never really disappear. I call them life stripes."

"How about bulging, distended anal veins?"

"No! Will you quit reading that stuff?"

Yet I couldn't help myself, despite the fact that two key elements of my personality did not exactly harmonize with the whole birth process. One is that I am deeply squeamish. Years ago I was channel flipping and chanced upon once of those "miracle of life" home-birth films. I think I moaned more than the mother-to-be as I watched with horrified fascination, unable to rip my eyes away from the screen. When the baby finally gushed forth, covered in what appeared to be tomato sauce, mozzarella cheese, and a liberal sprinkling of Parmesan, I gasped for air. As the doctor sawed through the ropy blue umbilical cord, I had to put my head between my legs while simultaneously scrambling to turn off the remote control.

Being a fiction writer with a runaway imagination was perhaps an even bigger impediment to motherhood. At night I lay awake in my bed as dark visions bloomed in my head like stinking nightshade.

Scenario one: As the nurse hands me the new baby, I clutch the newborn's head a little too eagerly and my blundering fingers punch through the soft spot on its skull. I am grasping the baby's head like a bowling ball. "Somebody help me!" I scream as the hospital staff backs away.

Scenario two: "They found her," Tom says in a voice hoarse from sleepless nights and worry. "She's been turning tricks in a bus station."

Scenario three: "I hate you, Mom and Dad!" screams our teenage son, his pupils spiraling from the drugs coursing through his system. He punches the air a few menacing inches from my head. (This scene was taken directly from a 1977 TV movie I once saw called *The Death of Richie*. Based on a true story that ran in *Life* magazine, it starred Ben Gazzara as a well-meaning parent whose son, played by Robby Benson, sank into harrowing drug addiction. At the end of the movie, Ben had to shoot his gibbering, violently out-of-control son in self-defense. That movie may have been single-handedly responsible for my fear of having kids.)

"Don't be weird," Tom would plead when I relayed these scenes to him. And mostly I was able to tamp down my paranoia after I noted how eagerly Tom had plunged into the next phase of our lives, humming to himself around the house as he gathered research on the safest car seat and the best prenatal vitamins. He ordered a night-light shaped like an elephant. He treated me like a piece of fragile Dresden porcelain, even when I was barely showing.

Best of all, he cooked me anything I wanted. I've always had the supreme luxury of having a husband who genuinely loves to cook. Tom is the sort of person who has always thought it was "fun," not dreary and time-consuming, to make refried beans from scratch or tackle an obscure Korean dish with thirty ingredients. He has a library of cookbooks from every land, and for years

I eagerly looked forward to the end of every afternoon when we discussed what was on the menu for dinner.

But after I found out I was pregnant, I suddenly acquired a new power. "You know what I'd like?" I mentioned once as I leafed through a Mario Batali cookbook. "Green maltagliati with oven-dried tomatoes, basil, and black-pepper mascarpone." I wasn't even sure what maltagliati was, but it looked mighty tasty in the picture, and Tom had just purchased a pasta-making machine.

He looked at the recipe, his eyebrows drawing together. "Hm," he said. "It looks kind of elaborate."

"Okay," I said, sighing—but quietly, because I knew better than to get peevish when someone was offering to cook me a meal.

Tom looked at me anxiously. "Unless you're having some sort of craving?"

I had never been troubled by the slightest pregnancy craving. All of my friends told stories of uncontrollable urges for heretofore-ignored foods. My mother inhaled banana Popsicles while she was carrying me and then never touched another after I was born. Heather wolfed down crunchy Cheez Doodles and then buried the bags in the bottom of the trash. I never had a craving for anything specific.

I smiled. "Funny you should say that. I've had such a hankering for"—I glanced down at the recipe—"mascarpone cheese. That's why I stopped on this recipe. But I understand, it's a little elaborate—"

"No, no, no," he said. "I'm happy to make it. Your body probably needs the calcium."

Soon enough, the fetus was ordering up elaborate, absurdly specific meals: sautéed chicken Chengdu-style ("I guess the poor little thing needs the protein," I said), braised short ribs ("I must be short on iron, don't you think?"), and Thai roasted-peanut noodles ("I was up half the night thinking about them, it's the *craziest* thing, it's just out of my control").

I was also able to get him to tidy up our apartment, which had always been a major source of marital wrangling. Tom has maintained that he is comforted by his many towering piles of books and periodicals and papers and letters and research. He feels they lend the place a scholarly feel and dreads tossing out anything—from a college term paper to a water-stained paperback bought from a street vendor—just in case he might "need it someday." I, on the other hand, hail from a compulsively neat family and abhor even a shred of clutter. I race to recycle any paper product the moment I am finished with it. If I lived alone, my apartment would contain a bed, a plate, and a fork.

For years, I begged Tom to declutter, especially after I read that silverfish love to burrow into old magazines and books. I was tormented by the idea of opening up an old novel and having a silverfish spring out into my lap. Not that I was sure silverfish even sprang, but that's how I envisioned it. But the most I could get Tom to do was to toss magazines that were over five years old.

That is, until I came across research on the nesting instinct that frequently kicked in among pregnant women, resulting in a frenzy of housecleaning. When Tom was able to assign my insane behavior to ancient biological forces rather than simply an annoying personality quirk, he was more apt to actually toss his dusty files of research for articles he had written during the Clinton administration. Harmony reigned in the household.

Breaking the news to my friend Lou was not quite as harmonious. For years, we had commiserated when some of our friends had had children and promptly disappeared. Now I had crossed over. When I told him, he said, "Oh my God! That's so great!" Then, deadpan: "Nice knowing you."

"Why do you say that?"

He sighed. "Because you're going to vanish. I feel like unless I get pregnant, too, you'll forget me. There is not one woman in the history of pregnant chicks who does not become a different person after having a child."

"But maybe different isn't all bad," I pointed out. "Maybe they become kinder and more empathetic."

"It's a gradual thing," he continued gloomily, as if he hadn't heard me. "As the belly gets bigger, the calls get fewer. And after the baby's born, you're never going to see that person alone. You're not going to go to a movie with them, or to dinner, and you can only talk on the phone when the baby is in bed and the parent is already exhausted. And the only visit granted is if you come to them and look at the kid. They're cute and it's fun to hold them, but the entire visit is all about the child—what they do, what foods they spit up."

"I'll still see you alone. Haven't you heard of day care?"

"You'll get amnesia. The kids suck the previous personality out of the parent until they have no recollection—remember when Brooke Adams fell asleep in *Invasion of the Body Snatchers* and the tendrils came out? The kids are like those pod things, with the tendrils." He paused. "I really am happy for you, but it's always like a little death when I hear the news. I just have to prepare myself."

I hung up, feeling morose. Surely I wouldn't fade away. Well, not everyone was going to react the way my family did, or Julie. When I phoned her, she choked up immediately. "Oh, Jancee," she said, her voice tight. "That is the most *wonderful news.* Wait until I tell Paul. Wait until I tell my mother. I know you're probably a little scared, but I'm telling you that you are going to love it." She sniffed. "I know you. Don't I know you? You trust me, right?

Oh! Just wait until the baby is six months. Six months to two years is the cutest age in the world. No, they all are. Some people say that the twos are difficult, or the threes, but I've loved every age. You will, too. And just wait—everyone is so nice to you when you're pregnant. Strangers smile at you and give you seats on the bus and the subway. Of course, when you actually have the baby, they make you stand from One Hundred Twenty-fifth Street to Coney Island. But that's a long way off."

Julie was right. Being pregnant transformed the city into a small town. As I swelled, people beamed at me in the street. Strangers really did leap up to offer me their seats. Yet it was still somewhat of an abstract concept until I had my third ultrasound, when the baby was much bigger and I would learn the gender. Tom was at a meeting he couldn't break, but I would see him at home in two hours and tell him the news.

The sonogram technician had dealt with me before and knew I was a little strange. I didn't ask her the standard questions, for one thing.

"What's with people sending mass emails of their sonogram pictures?" I said as she rubbed some goo on my stomach. "I have friends who send them to everyone at work."

"I don't know," she said. "It's the thing to do now."

"But isn't it jumping the gun a little? Plus those head-on shots have a sort of 'grinning skull' look that's not exactly cute and cuddly. Am I right?" She nodded and told me about an artist, popular in New York City, who actually colored in the sonogram photos and made them more lifelike. *Yeesh.* I begged her to get me his name so I could write a story about it.

"Don't you have any questions about the baby?" she asked gently. "Look right here," she said, pointing at a place on the monitor. "Do you see the baby's eyes? Isn't that exciting?"

"You mean the sockets," I said darkly. "I just see blackness. See? Sockets. I don't think the baby has eyes. The baby is missing its eyes."

She looked at me with concern. "Of course the baby has eyes. Look there. Right there. These are the lenses."

"Oh," I said. "Now I see."

She grinned. "Do you want to know the gender?"

I did.

"It's a girl! Congratulations."

A girl! I secretly wanted a girl. I felt a flood of tenderness for the little fetus. Look at how lively she was, leaping around like a tiny Mexican jumping bean! Suddenly it all became real. She was real.

"Would you like me to print out some of the sonogram photos?"

"Yes," I said jubilantly. "Would you mind getting me the one of her profile? She has Tom's nose."

I hurried home with my sonogram photos, and when I told Tom we were having a daughter, he hugged me tightly. "Now I have two girls to love," he said.

I called Julie and excitedly told her the news. "I knew it," she said. "I knew it was going to be a girl. Isn't it funny that we both will have one daughter? Another thing we have in common! I just thought of something. Let me call you right back."

Five minutes later, she phoned me. "I talked to my mother," she said. "I've been saving all of Violet's clothes at her house and she's going to bring them to my place. Originally I was going to give them to my brother, but for some reason he never got them. It's fate. It's fate!" A week later, she invited me to come over to her apartment to "pick up a few things." When I got there, she was waiting in the lobby with a luggage trolley she had commandeered from the superintendent. Piled on the trolley were eight bulging contractor bags stuffed full of maternity clothes, baby outfits, and toddler clothes. "You're all set," Julie announced triumphantly.

Back at my apartment, after I spent an entire weekend sorting through the colorful mountain of clothes, I remembered to mail my folks a copy of our sonogram photos.

"I'm not sending these things to anyone but our parents," I told Tom, putting a stamp on the envelope. "But I think they'll get a kick out of them."

Indeed they did, and when I went to visit my parents a few weeks later, they proudly led me to the living room. "Come see what we did," said my mother. She pointed to our trove of family pictures displayed on a table. Nestled among them was a framed photo of one of the sonogram pictures, a profile shot of the baby's head.

"She fits right in," noted my father. Admittedly, her face looked a little eerie next to the faces of the family members who had actual skin, but I was still touched.

17

I'm Gettin' a Tattoo

Last Thanksgiving, right about the time that our family had finished scraping up the remainder of our triple fleet of pies (pecan, chocolate, and pumpkin), my mother pushed away from the table, dabbed her lips with a napkin, and calmly made an announcement.

"I'm gettin' a tattoo," she said.

All of us froze. Most even stopped chewing, a testament to the gravity of the situation.

She looked around, defiant. "I've been thinking about this for a long time. I'm doing it, and that's that."

Our dining table, strewn with artificial pumpkins and votive candles in harvest colors, suddenly transformed into a hushed, packed courtroom. Nobody spoke.

I cleared my throat. "Mom," I said finally. "Mom. You're not a kid. You're __. (Note: I have been requested not to reveal the exact number, as she looks considerably more youthful than her calendar age and would prefer to "let people wonder.")

Dinah's fork hovered motionless over the last scrap of her chocolate pie. "What do you plan to get, exactly?" she asked in a faint voice.

My mother drew herself up, relishing the moment. "I've decided to get a raven."

"Why?" Dinah still hadn't resumed eating. I had already polished off my chocolate pie and wondered if I could finish hers, provided that she cut away the parts her fork had touched.

My mother shrugged. "I don't know why. I've always liked ravens. Maybe that's my totem or something, I don't know. They just appeal to me."

"I think I need to be fanned," I heard Heather mutter to her husband, Rob. Then she asked my mother where she planned to have this tattoo inscribed.

"On my wrist," she replied, waving her left hand over what I felt was a very large area of her right wrist.

Dinah tried again. "Is this some sort of midlife thing?"

My mother laughed. "I've passed midlife. Am I having a later-in-life crisis? No. I just think it's going to make me happy."

Then I stepped in. "You'll get tired of looking at it, believe me. Don't you get sick of your clothes, your jewelry? You go out and buy new ones and give the old ones to Goodwill. Well, you can't do that with tattoos. Simon Doonan once called them 'permanent bell-bottoms.'"

At the same moment, we all arrived at the collective realization that my father had not yet said a word. Every head snapped to where he sat at the long table opposite Mom. His resigned expression made it clear that they had already chewed the issue over.

Heather frowned. "Dad? You have nothing to say?"

He sighed and put down his fork. "Well," he began finally. "I wish she wouldn't do it, because it's not easy to reverse those things. Your mother is a beautiful woman. Why be a human billboard?"

My dad shook his head. "But you know your mother. The more you protest, the more determined she is to do it. When I object heavily to something, she'll get her back up. I gave her my opinion, and either she takes it or she doesn't. I respect her decision if that's what she wants to do, but I don't agree with it. Styles come and go. What's it going to look like when she's all wrinkled up? You're not going to be able to tell what the hell it is. I don't know, a butterfly on the wrist?"

"Didn't you hear her?" said Heather. "She wants a raven."

My dad grunted. "Hm. Even worse. A black raven? That's kind of dark, isn't it? It will just look like a liver spot gone wild."

My mom laughed merrily. "It's my body," she said. "I do not understand why everyone is getting so upset."

I raised my eyebrows and informed her that had I floated the idea of a tattoo for myself ten years ago, she would not have approved.

She nodded. "That's true. I think ten years ago you would have been too young to decide something that was permanent. At my age, I'm certainly more aware that this is something I want for the rest of my life." My mother's little announcement would have been considerably less jarring if I had the sort of parents some of my friends had, ones who smoked pot with their kids or strolled around the house nude or passed on their treasured collection of Hendrix records. But my folks had always been unapologetically square.

I tried for levity. "If you're going to be radical, why not go all the way? Get a tattoo that fools the eye. How about a port-wine stain? Or give yourself a chin cleft."

"Why not lengthen your butt crack halfway up your back?" said Heather. "That would freak out everyone in your garden club."

Tom cleared his throat. "Some senior citizens have gotten tattoos saying 'Do not resuscitate,'" he pointed out. "Just an option."

The laughter faded and we stared at our plates while my mother dug with gusto into the remainder of her pie. I could tell she was feeling pretty satisfied with herself. Rob, who has age-appropriate tribal tattoos of his own, jumped up to bring out more decaf coffee and to remove himself from the awkwardness. We all watched him intently as he poured it into our mugs. "Well," I said at length. "If you're going to go through with it, will you at least allow me to choose the place you go to? I have friends who have gotten tattoos, and I don't want you going to some fly-by-night joint."

"Sure," said my mom, nodding. "Sure."

"In fact," I went on, "a crony of mine just wrote an article on the best tattoo artists in New York City. They're the ones who work on various celebrities. They don't come cheap, but then again, I suppose this is a pretty important decision."

Dinah and Heather looked at me, their eyes widening with incredulity and then narrowing. I knew I'd hear about it later.

The moment arrived after dinner, as I settled into my parents' guest room wearing a pair of my mother's pale yellow Liz Claiborne sweats. Tom was downstairs playing video soccer with Rob, and I was gearing up to flip through a pile of my mother's *Southern Living* magazines. I could not get enough of their demented recipes, my favorite so far being a turtle trifle, which involves cutting a pecan pie into cubes and layering it in a trifle dish with mascarpone cheese, fudge sauce, caramel sauce, and more pecans. That's it. (I laugh, but would I eat it? Oh yes.)

And it seemed to be an editorial mandate that each issue contain some variation of a recipe for corn bread—corn-bread crêpes, open-faced shrimp corn-bread sandwiches. Ah. Here we go: corn-bread croutons. *Hm,* I thought absently. *I might eat that. A little heavy, sure, but—*

A loud knock interrupted my thoughts, and Dinah and Heather burst in without an invitation. They both took a seat on the bed.

I looked at them. "Did you notice we're all wearing Liz Claiborne sweats? What, did Mom just pass them out to everyone? They have a weird way of making us look shorter, don't you think?"

They wouldn't be distracted. Heather got right into it. "You know what, Jancee? I think you're an enabler."

"You are," Dinah put in. "You made the whole process seem fun, like, 'Let's go to New York City and have a crazy day in the East Village, getting a tattoo.'"

"Whoa," I said. "Why are you people turning on me? I think this is a horrible idea, too."

"You know why?" said Dinah. "If we hadn't started screaming, this might have gone away. If you hadn't turned it into this grand adventure where you take her to New York, then she wouldn't do it. It's all about attention. I know Claire's only five, but I've already thought about this: When she comes to tell me she's going to pierce her nose, I'm not even going to look up from my book."

Heather smirked. "I hate to tell you, Dinah, but if she's going to pierce her nose, all she needs is a bathroom, rubbing alcohol, and an earring."

Dinah ignored her and kept her eyes trained on me. "And of course you're excited about this announcement because you're going to write about it. I mean, come on. We're not dumb."

I acknowledged that for a writer always on the hunt for material, this was a gift sent straight from heaven on a fluffy pink cloud.

Dinah shook her head. "You know what this is? It's clichéd rebellion," she said. "I don't want to think about it. I don't want to think this way about Mom. It's rare that I don't think the things she does are pretty great. Usually she's so sure of herself, and I don't know, this one I don't understand."

Heather flopped back grumpily onto my pillows. "The tattoo will clash with her radish pin." My mother had a few garden-themed pins shaped like vegetables. "I'm just not amused. It's silly. If she gets a tattoo, I don't even want to look at it. This doesn't deserve any more talk." She folded her arms. "Case closed."

Yet we continued to chew it over. Traditionally after holiday gatherings, one of our bedrooms becomes a post-dinner salon where the night's events are dissected. Before my mother made her announcement, the *scandale de la nuit* was shaping up to be my father's weird show of temper at dinner when my mother mentioned that she wanted to update the family photos in the dining room. He preferred for them to stay forever frozen in the Carter era, when my mother sported a frizzy perm à la Barbra Streisand's in the remake of *A Star Is Born* ("the best your mother ever looked," my father would claim to stunned silence). When my father banged his hand on the table and bellowed that the photos weren't changing, we sisters primed for a juvenile late-night "What the hell is up with Dad and his freaky outburst" discussion. At least an hour could have been wrung from it, from speculation on the general state of our parents' marriage to crafting a plan to tell Mom to inform Dad not to flip out at the dinner table.

But our mother's harebrained scheme had bumped every other issue off the agenda. "Why does this make me so uncomfortable?" I asked my sisters. "It must be her age."

Dinah shook her head. "It's not that I think older women

shouldn't get tattoos. I just don't think it fits Mom. It's the same reason I don't want one for myself. It's a personality issue."

"I agree," I said. "She's not the sort of mom that Cher played in *Mask,* when she rode around on the back of a motorcycle. She's a different type."

"Eventually, her skin will be sagging," said Heather. "And so will the crow."

"It's a raven," I said.

"Whatever. I just don't want to see her lying in a coffin with a crow tattoo on her wrist."

"It's a raven."

"Whatever. Mom is a confident, beautiful—"

"Smart person," put in Dinah.

"And this is like her wearing—"

"Hot pants," finished Dinah.

We sat quietly. "Here's an idea," I said. "What if we had her get it in a place that's more discreet than her wrist?"

"She's not going to get it," Heather declared. "She isn't. What's the fun of getting it if your daughters won't go with you? Because guess what, I'm not going with her. I'm not."

"What if we encouraged her to do it on her ankle?" I said.

"No!" said Heather, her mouth a firm line. "It's still there. She's walking around in the backyard picking hydrangeas to put in a vase, and she's got this dark splotch on her leg."

Dinah nodded. "If it was something for her that was private, that's a whole different thing. Tell her that we'd be much happier if she got it in a place where we couldn't see it."

"Ever," said Heather.

But when I approached my mother in the kitchen the next morning and floated the idea of an ankle tattoo, the woman wouldn't budge. "I want to be able to see it, like a wristwatch," she said, sticking a leftover Pillsbury crescent roll into the toaster oven and taking a container of I Can't Believe It's Not Butter! spray out of the fridge. I told her she would contract hepatitis. She placidly sprayed the crescent roll without acknowledging me.

Defeated, I went back to my apartment and plunged like a private detective into researching the seamy world of tattoos. I learned that over a third of Americans between the ages of eighteen and twenty-five now had a tattoo. Perhaps getting inked wasn't so seamy after all; a store called Tattoo Nation opened in 2006 at the Woodbridge Center mall in New Jersey (the first of what the owners planned to be an eventual four hundred stores nationwide).

I reckoned that if my mother was going to go through with this loony decision, she might as well get the best artist available. I consulted my friend's article, "The City's Top Inkers." The horror and Goth specialist beloved by bands like Slayer and Pantera might not be quite right, but I did find one who had given Rosie O'Donnell a tat. That would excite my mother, a Rosie fan, for sure.

Unfortunately the waiting list for him was seven months. Another famous tattoo artist told me he was booked up for the entire year. So I trolled through tattoo magazines and websites in search of artists who were not quite as well known but still skilled. I waded through hundreds of portfolios and beheld every design imaginable covering a parade of flabby forearms, hairy backs, and bikini lines that no bikini had ever graced. I spent whole afternoons getting lost in the many ways one can decorate one's body: crying Rottweilers, a crying mime's mask, and a preponderance of tattoos on people's stomachs featuring the rear ends of animals, tail up, cleverly using the person's navel as the butt opening. Every possible celebrity has been permanently committed to someone's skin: Christopher Walken, an elderly Bob Barker, Patrick Swayze as a centaur in a sleeveless Chippendales tuxedo with a double-helix rainbow behind him. *Maddox Jolie-Pitt,* for God's sake.

It was hard to accept that my mother was aiming to join this particular club. When I told an artist friend of mine that she was going under the needle, he immediately said, "Wow—that's so awesome. You should support her."

"Yes, but would it be as awesome if your own mother did it?"

He thought for a moment. "You know, I guess not." That's the thing: It was awesome if it was someone else's mother.

My investigation of New York City tattoo parlors continued apace. I had come to accept that the tattoo artist would have a name like Snake or Double Z or Pit Bull or Whitey and would likely moonlight in a band (one artist's band was called A Day of Pigs). But I didn't want the actual place to be so freakily alternative that my mother would be unnerved, so that knocked out a lot of venues on Avenue C and the more hipster-clogged regions of Williamsburg. Something a bit more mainstream was called for.

Yet I could not find any senior-lady-friendly establishments. You would think a tattoo parlor for the Eileen Fisher demographic would have cropped up by now, with cheery daffodil walls and free pots of decaf coffee and day care for the grandkids while tattoos are applied.

Perhaps a New Jersey–based establishment would make her feel slightly more at home. Again I went to the Internet and spent a weekend hunched over my computer, narrowing down a list of candidates, before finally deciding on Shotsie's Tattoo of Wayne, New Jersey. My father had probably passed the place many times on his way to the JC Penney store he managed in the same town. The website was reassuringly welcoming ("Why not stop in and say hi? I'm sure you will feel very comfortable here and we can discuss all your tattooing needs and concerns"). *Hi,* I pictured myself telling the owner. *I'm concerned that my mother is halfway around the bend. Mind if I pull up a chair?*

I saw that the place opened at 1 P.M. on weekdays. Maybe if we went on, say, a Tuesday, right at opening time, no one else would be there. I reckoned that most tattoo seekers would venture in at night. If I were being honest, my anxiety was more about my own comfort than my mother's. I was privately relieved that we weren't going to Avenue C. I wanted desperately to hustle her quietly in the back door, like a celebrity getting a secret brow lift at the plastic surgeon.

I was particularly drawn to the designs of a tattoo artist called "the Ink Shrink." So I dialed Shotsie's to ask him a few questions, running over to my stereo first to turn off the classical music station that was playing in the background.

"Hi, is the Ink Shrink in, by chance?"

"Who's that?" said a voice. "We don't have anyone by that name."

I began to sweat lightly. "Well, it says on your website that you do, and—"

"Hold on." I heard him holler to someone in another room. "Christopher? Do you call yourself the Ink Shrink?" Back to me. "Okay, yeah, he's here. What do you want to talk to him about?"

"My mother wants a tattoo," I said miserably. "Can I just ask him a few quick questions?"

Christopher got on the phone and I explained the situation, still sweating. "Do you work on old people?" I asked.

"How old?"

I told him.

"Is she healthy?"

"Yes."

"Shouldn't be a problem then," said Christopher. He seemed like an amiable guy. I asked him the protocol, and he told me that she should come in first for a consultation so he would know how long to book for the job.

"Listen," I said, "she wants to get a tattoo of a raven on her wrist. I was wondering if you could maybe steer her in the direction of her ankle during this consultation."

He thought for a moment. "Well, no, I don't think so. The wrist is a popular spot now. If it's done right, which is what I do, it will look beautiful."

"The thing is, I keep trying to tell her she should get it on her ankle. Then she can cover it up if she wants."

"Well, at this point, she doesn't really have to listen to you, does she?"

"I guess not."

He laughed. "She sounds like a cool lady. Tell her to come in." In the meantime I received this email from a friend:

> That guy Shotsie was like, a tattoo legend in NJ (you probably know this). I remember all the NY hardcore bands apparently went to Shotsie back in the day (because I think tattooing was illegal in NYC for many years but was legal in NJ). So your mom is in the great company of NJ hardcore and death metal bands from that time. You should ask the people there about it.

Well. That was some good news.

And so my mother, after responsibly vetting Shotsie's with the Better Business Bureau for any violations (none found), made a consultation appointment with the Ink Shrink for the following Saturday.

"I suppose I'd be open to another area rather than the wrist," she mused beforehand. "I want to talk to this Ink Shrink to find out the best place to put it. I don't want the tattoo to droop."

Guess what, lady, I thought. *It's going to droop no matter where you put it.* Where was this magical, perpetually firm spot on the wrist? Maybe she was thinking beyond, to her palms. Or another non-drooping area altogether, like the roof of her mouth or the top of her skull.

"You know you can still back out, right?" I told her, adding that my pious Russian cleaning lady, Luba, was horrified when I told her the news. When Luba next visited to clean my apartment, she brought along her well-thumbed Bible and said she had something to show me. "Look," she said, leafing through it until she arrived at Leviticus 20:28. She had me read the verse aloud: "You shall not make any cuttings in your flesh for the dead, nor print any marks upon you: I *am* the Lord."

Luba looked at me gravely. "Tell Mama God says not to do it."

I repeated this dictum from the world's highest authority to my mother, but she just laughed.

That Saturday afternoon, post-consultation, I received the inevitable joint phone call from the folks to report back. They called from the car as they pulled onto Route 23.

"Everyone that worked there had studs in every orifice and tattoos on every piece of skin," said my father. "It looked like Fright Night in the Village. Then there was us. Hell, we were the only two shocking people there. We felt like two narcs."

"You don't say."

"It wasn't intimidating," said my mother. "We were just out of our element." My stomach contracted as I pictured my mom in her spring-green jacket from Talbots and my dad with his friendly, open smile. Should that not have been a sign that she was doing the wrong thing? Why were they there?

"The receptionist was even whiter than you," my mother continued. As a white girl with Scottish roots and an aversion to sun, I had skin the bluish color of irradiated skim milk. "I mean her face was totally pale, no color whatsoever, and she had dyed black hair." I wasn't listening because I was still stuck on *receptionist*. Did tattoo parlors have receptionists?

"I don't think it was dyed," said my father.

"Yes it was." While they argued about her precise hair color, I returned to the shoe website I had been perusing before they called. Finally they moved on to the Ink Shrink, a.k.a. Christopher DePinto, who was heavily tattooed but "extremely pleasant," said my mother. "He said 'awesome' a lot."

My mother showed him some of her favorite designs that he had instructed her to download and print out. Then he told her he'd make up a stencil, and vetoed her plan of swilling wine during the procedure, as alcohol thins your blood. My mother asked him if the process would hurt.

I returned wearily to the shoe website because I knew exactly what my father was going to say next. And indeed: "I told Christopher, 'She's been through childbirth, for God's sake,'" said my dad.

I grew more dyspeptic as I pictured my parents making bright, chirpy conversation with hip, nocturnal Christopher. I went to my bathroom and rummaged in the cabinet for the antacids.

"All in all, I think we provided a lot of conversation for the employees after we left," said my father ruefully.

"Well, Dad? How do you feel? Better? Worse? Reassured?"

"Yes," he said. "I think this is so unnecessary that I can't stand it. But I'm through talking to her about the whole thing." He was genuinely aggrieved that she was going through with it. I understood.

And so a month later, on a drizzly gray day in December, I headed back to New Jersey to watch my mother get inked. I had begged Heather to come along, but that morning she had phoned me and said she couldn't go.

"I contracted some sort of eye infection yesterday," she said miserably. "I went to the doctor and he had no idea what it was. In fact, he was so amazed by it that he took pictures of me to show to other doctors. I was a big hit."

"That's reassuring. Did he ask you if you had been swimming in any South American rivers?"

She managed a weak laugh. "So now my eye is oozing. I'm also wearing an eye patch."

"That's even better," I said. "You'll give our little group a much-needed edge. It will offset Mom's Talbots sweater and my pregnancy waddling. I'm wearing an open puffer coat because I can't close it over my belly. You'll make us look hip. In fact, stop by Bird World on the way and get a parrot to put on your shoulder. It'll boost the freak factor."

"I can't. I'm so sorry. I'm really in pain." I didn't have the heart to push her.

Dinah was working, so I headed off by myself. My parents had decided to make an occasion of it, so we met first at Hunan Taste, our favorite Chinese restaurant. Hunan Taste was gold and red and shaped like a huge pagoda, and it had a koi pond both outside and inside its entrance. I loved its mixture of glitz and grandeur. The waiters wore tuxes, and the restaurant was divided into two rooms separated by enormous saltwater fish tanks, so that as you ate your pork dumplings with spicy peanut sauce, you could watch the fish. Even the top of the bar was a Plexiglas fish tank, so goldfish swam placidly underneath your drink.

As my mother dug into her dumplings, she told us about a dream she had had the night before, in which she was drawing various tattoo designs on her wrist. "And I remember trying out the idea of two eyes and thinking, *Huh, that's interesting.*" She grinned at us. "Wouldn't it be interesting to have two eyes on your wrist?"

My father opened his mouth and then closed it, while I tried to keep my face composed. "It would be interesting," I said mildly. "Here's another idea: How about one eye on each wrist?" I sighed. "Wouldn't you feel guilty every time you sprayed perfume on your wrist, right into those open eyes? Mom, could you please have mercy on us? We just got used to the raven." I leaned in. "I still haven't figured out why, exactly, you're doing this. You said you were too old to rebel. So I'm thinking you're doing it for attention."

She signaled the waiter for more rice. "No, I am not," she said. "I don't care if anyone else sees it. I don't."

My father found his voice. "Then why are you putting it on your wrist?"

"So *I* can see it! Why can't you both believe that there's no other reason than simply that I want it?"

I looked at her. "Because there's always a reason."

She rolled her eyes. "Why must there be some dark, hidden psychological explanation for every behavior? Jesus Christ! Your generation is so analytical. Honestly, y'all have had way too much therapy. I want to get it because it's art. It's art on my body. It's like creating your own painting. That's it."

Dad consulted his watch and did some silent calculations. "Twenty minutes. Let's get the check. We don't want to be late."

Shotsie's was a small, square building off of Route 23. As we walked through the door, "Sure Shot" from the Beastie Boys was blaring from the speakers. "I interviewed them," I told my father. "They were a little difficult." My father nodded politely.

The tattooed young guy at reception told us that Christopher would be right out, so the three of us sat on the couch and flipped through a pile of tattoo books for some last-minute inspiration. A heart with UGLY & PROUD written across it, perhaps? Or—here's one—an expanse of flesh slit open, forming a bloody gash stuffed with eyeballs?

Then out came Christopher, who greeted us with a big smile and a wink for me. He led us to his workroom, a dark lair with a black glossy floor, steel walls, and what appeared to be a brain in a jar of formaldehyde. His arms were covered in tattoos. He had spiked hair, a spiked belt, and a spiked black backpack tossed near his chair.

He and my mother plotted out the design, a raven with black lines and gray and white shading. My father lingered uncertainly in the doorway while I took a seat on Christopher's leather couch and discreetly tucked away the magazine that poked out of my purse, the *Martha Stewart Living* Christmas cookie issue, with a page marked for the peanut-toffee-chip bars I planned to make.

I willed myself not to tell him that I used to work at *Rolling Stone*. An inner voice warned me, *Please, please don't try to establish your street cred. First of all,* Rolling Stone *isn't exactly hip anymore, and even if it was, you stopped working there years ago.*

"I used to work at *Rolling Stone* magazine," I blurted. "I guess a lot of hard-core bands have come here, huh?"

He nodded as he fitted a design prototype on my mother's wrist. The raven was placed off-center, as if it were going to fly away.

"I like the idea of it taking off," said my mother.

I asked Christopher, a former piercer who had graduated to tattoos, how many tats he had, and he said he had no idea. "After a while it just turns into one big one," he said with a shrug. Then I wanted to know if he ever turned anyone down, and he nodded. "If I sense a certain kind of apprehension," he said. "If there are questions about removal right away. Or if the design they want is crap, or a bad idea. You know, you can't get *The Last Supper* as a toe ring."

My father nodded solemnly.

Then Christopher asked my mother if she was ready. She looked so small as she sat in the treatment chair. She said she was as ready as she'd ever be, and Christopher pulled on a pair of purple rubber gloves. I looked over at my father and knew that his queasy, fretful expression matched my own. "Okey-dokey," said Christopher.

Then there was quiet except for the buzzing of the needle.

My mother stayed admirably calm. "Well, it's not pleasant, but I don't feel like screaming," she said after a moment.

Dad gave me a tight smile. "Don't take it personally, but we fought this tooth and nail," he told Christopher. "She's not the normal demographic."

Christopher shrugged. "You'd be surprised," he said. "It's all different now."

Then, with the knowledge that there was no turning back, my father relaxed a little and began to pepper Christopher with Retiree Dad questions: So, are you a subcontractor here or a salaried employee? Do you enter tattoo competitions? Have you ever been to Hunan Taste? Excellent Chinese food; very high-quality. Then, emboldened by Christopher's chatty answers, my father drew from his lengthy street experience of watching *The Wire* and *Oz* and asked if he had ever seen tattoos made by prisoners.

"Sure. The guys are very innovative. I've never seen a quality tattoo, but I've seen real artistry, given their limited equipment. The best was one that was made with nothing but a guitar string and melted checkers."

"You know, you should go to my daughter's website," said my father, now fully comfortable. "Lots of really cute stuff, and boy, is it funny. She has—"

"Dad." I silenced him with a warning look.

After an hour, the tattoo was almost done. "I still don't really have a reason why I chose a raven," my mother said to Christopher.

"Mm," he said, applying the final bits of white to the wings. "Well, they collect meaning. You may say, 'I just like it,' but I'll bet in five years you'll have more insight." He wiped her wrist. "There," he said.

He did a good job. The raven, about two and a half inches long, looked light and delicate, almost feminine. I supposed that like everything else, I would get used to it. My mother turned her wrist back and forth, admiring the design. "I love it," she said. "I absolutely love it." And that was that. My mother didn't like a lot of fanfare. Then she announced that she had to use the ladies' room.

"Your mom is awesome," Christopher said to me as she left the room. I told him he was pretty awesome himself. I could have kissed him for the way he was so kind and solicitous to my folks.

After I paid the tab, the day's least hip moment occurred— certainly no mean feat—when my father pulled out his camera. "How about a picture?" he said jovially. He led Christopher outside to the front of the store and stuck him between my mom and me.

"Okay, gang!" my dad said cheerily, as if we were at Hersheypark. "Big smile!"

And then, just to sand off any remaining edge that I might have once possessed, we all headed over to the nearby JC Penney store where my father had been manager; he wanted to see how the Christmas merchandise was moving. He gave me a playful shove. "And maybe you can check out the maternity fashions! Right, kid?"

As my mother happily waved good-bye to everyone at Shotsie's, it became obvious that it had been I who was incredibly un-comfortable, not my mother. She never tried to be anything other than exactly who she was. I was the aging hipster who was queasy about my expandable maternity pants and sensible flat shoes and preference for classical music. It was a poignant trip for me, not her, because back in the day, I had probably interviewed a good number of the metal and punk bands who had gotten inked at Shotsie's. As I said my own good-byes to the gaggle of twenty-something Shotsie's employees, it seemed that I was surrounded by the fish-belly-pale, sylph-like, black-clad ghosts of my younger self. Just as I bid adieu to my own youth, my mother took hers up. Go figure.

I heaved my pumpkin-shaped body into the backseat of my parents' car and stared out the window as we drove toward JC Penney. I let my thoughts drift. *Today, I stood by helplessly as some-one I love did something that I thought was reckless and foolish, and when I tried to talk her out of it, she didn't listen to me for one second, even though I was certain I knew best.* It seemed that my mother had given me a handy preview of parenthood.

The next morning, safely back in my Brooklyn apartment, I heard the phone ring in my bedroom while I was in the shower. I checked the message and it was my mother:

Hi, Jancee. Thank you so much for helping me get that tattoo yes-terday. I was lookin' at it this morning, and I have to say, it makes me so happy. Listen, I really think you should get one, too. Just a little one, like maybe—"

I put my head in my hands. "I can't believe what I'm hearing!" I shouted to the machine, as my two cats pattered into the bed-room and stared at me, concerned.

She was still talking. —*another thing I've been thinking about is that I really feel like you should consider having two children.*

"The first one isn't even out of the oven yet!" I hollered. "Give it a rest, lady."

—just that you kids have brought me so much joy, and I want you to have the same thing, and— (strangled voice) *Each of you girls is my favorite child. Oh, hell, now I'm getting choked up. But really, think it over. Okay, I'm gonna go now. Talk to you soon.*

I sat down on my bed and sighed heavily.

"Please tell me I'm not as crazy as she is," I said to the cats.

ACKNOWLEDGMENTS

I must first thank my sisters, Dinah and Heather, without whom this book would not have been written. I phoned them both hundreds of times, and they were always kind and helpful, even when I called them during dinner and they were frantically trying to feed the kids. I am so lucky to have them.

My heartfelt gratitude to my husband, Tom, on whom I still have a schoolgirl crush after eight years of marriage.

I will always be grateful to the lovely Julie Klam, who makes me laugh every single day; to Jill Schwartzman, my beloved editor, whose keen intelligence and enthusiasm have inspired me once again; and to David McCormick, my agent for life.

At Random House/Villard, I'd also like to thank Jane von Mehren, Kim Hovey, Lisa Barnes, Sanyu Dillon, Brian McClendon, Bruce Tracy, Benjamin Dreyer, Beth Pearson, and Lea Beresford.

Most of all I must thank my parents, who have acquiesced with remarkable good cheer to having their every move documented in a book. I am often asked if they put up a fight when I take notes on their behavior. Sometimes they do, at which point I say that I need their cooperation, as I will likely be the one who foots the bill when they grow feeble. Then I calmly list their options. There is the Elder Care Platinum Package (a round-the-clock personal nurse installed comfortably in their own home), the Gold Package (free lodging in a senior-friendly cottage situated on the property of the country house I hope to buy one day), or the Silver Package (a top-of-the-line assisted-living facility).

Then I remind them that if they decide not to play ball and withhold those valuable nutty quotes, then my book will sell poorly and they face the Elder Care Economy Package: living in my sister Dinah's basement. Dinah has protested this arrangement in the past, but I've told her repeatedly that I live in a cramped New York City apartment without a basement, while she has a suburban house. Plus, old people shrink as they age, so the folks won't take up too much room. And Dinah won't have to pay any extra money, because she can be their round-the-clock nurse herself. See? It all works out.

This is the sort of difficult but necessary conversation that you must have with siblings when your parents get older. I'm just grateful we're all so close. Then it's less painful to sit down with your sister, look her in the eye, and say, *You do it. I don't want to. Taking care of old people isn't really my "thing."* That kind of comfort level—well, it's what family is all about.

About the Author

JANCEE DUNN grew up in Chatham, New Jersey. From 1989 to 2003, she was a staff writer at *Rolling Stone.* Her work has appeared in *GQ,* for which she wrote a monthly sex advice column; *Vogue; The New York Times;* and *O: The Oprah Magazine,* for which she writes a monthly ethics column. She has also been a VJ for MTV2 and an entertainment correspondent for *Good Morning America.* Dunn is the author of *But Enough About Me,* a 2006 memoir about her life as a chronically nervous celebrity interviewer, and *Don't You Forget About Me,* a novel released in 2008. She lives with her husband, the writer Tom Vanderbilt, in a converted church in Brooklyn, New York.